W9-AZV-371

studysync®

Reading & Writing Companion

What's Next?

How can we transform the future?

studysync.com

Copyright © BookheadEd Learning, LLC
All Rights Reserved.

Send all inquiries to:
BookheadEd Learning, LLC
610 Daniel Young Drive
Sonoma, CA 95476

No part of this publication may be reproduced or transmitted in any form, by any means, electronic or mechanical, including photocopy, recording, or utilized by any information storage or retrieval system, without written permission from BookheadEd Learning, LLC.

ISBN 978-1-94-973910-7

3 4 5 6 LMN 24 23 22 21 20

B

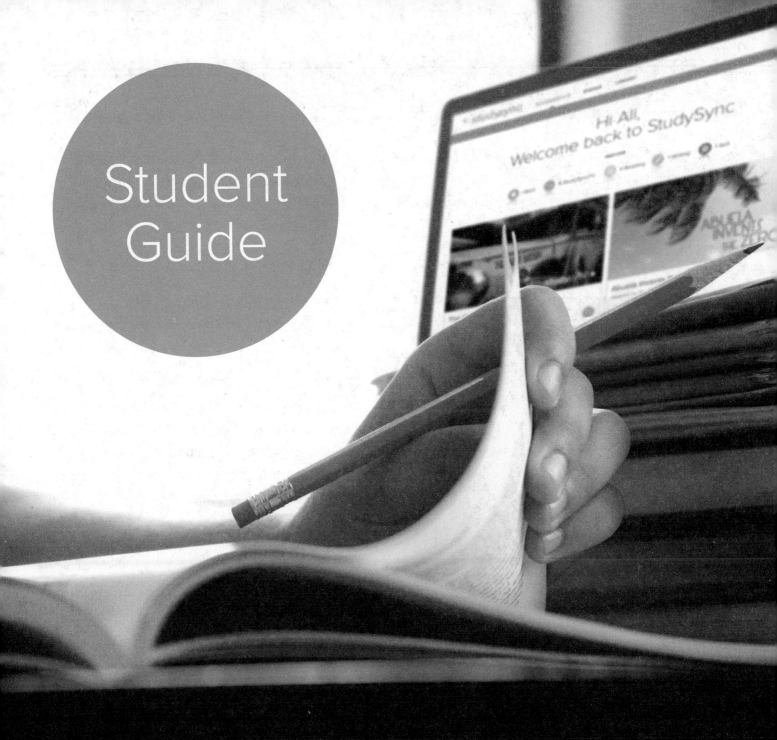

Student Guide

Getting Started

Welcome to the StudySync Reading & Writing Companion! In this book, you will find a collection of readings based on the theme of the unit you are studying. As you work through the readings, you will be asked to answer questions and perform a variety of tasks designed to help you closely analyze and understand each text selection. Read on for an explanation of each

Close Reading and Writing Routine

In each unit, you will read texts that share a common theme, despite their different genres, time periods, and authors. Each reading encourages a closer look through questions and a short writing assignment.

1 Introduction

An Introduction to each text provides historical context for your reading as well as information about the author. You will also learn about the genre of the text and the year in which it was written.

2 Notes

Many times, while working through the activities after each text, you will be asked to **annotate** or **make annotations** about what you are reading. This means that you should highlight or underline words in the text and use the "Notes" column to make comments or jot down any questions you have. You may also want to note any unfamiliar vocabulary words here.

You will also see sample student annotations to go along with the Skill lesson for that text.

Copyright © BookheadEd Learning, LLC

③ First Read

During your first reading of each selection, you should just try to get a general idea of the content and message of the reading. Don't worry if there are parts you don't understand or words that are unfamiliar to you. You'll have an opportunity later to dive deeper into the text.

④ Think Questions

These questions will ask you to start thinking critically about the text, asking specific questions about its purpose, and making connections to your prior knowledge and reading experiences. To answer these questions, you should go back to the text and draw upon specific evidence to support your responses. You will also begin to explore some of the more challenging vocabulary words in the selection.

⑤ Skills

Each Skill includes two parts: Checklist and Your Turn. In the Checklist, you will learn the process for analyzing the text. The model student annotations in the text provide examples of how you might make your own notes following the instructions in the Checklist. In the Your Turn, you will use those same instructions to practice the skill.

Copyright © BookheadEd Learning, LLC

---

③ First Read

Read "Are the New 'Golden Age' TV Shows the New Novels?" After you read, complete the Think Questions below.

④ ☁ THINK QUESTIONS

1. What does Kirsch say about how TV has changed recently? What is the "new genre" he mentions? Use evidence from the text to support your answer.

2. Why do people often compare "good" TV to the writing of Charles Dickens? What does Kirsch say about Dickens's writing that welcomes this comparison? Use evidence from the text to support your answer.

3. What are the reasons Hamid gives for watching more television than in the past? Use evidence from the text to support your answer.

4. What is the meaning of the word **capacious** as it is used in the text? Write your best definition here, along with a brief explanation of how you inferred its meaning through context.

5. Read the following dictionary entry:

   idiom
   id•i•om /ˈidēəm/ noun
   1. a group of words, that when used together, have an unclear meaning when read literally
   2. a form of expression natural to a language, person, or group of people
   3. the dialect of a people or part of a country
   4. a characteristic mode of expression in music, literature or art

   Which definition most closely matches the meaning of idiom as it is used in paragraph 4? Write the correct definition of idiom here and explain how you figured out its meaning.

---

⑤ Skill: Informational Text Elements

Use the Checklist to analyze Informational Text Elements in "Are the New 'Golden Age' TV Shows the New Novels?" Refer to the sample student annotations about Informational Text Elements in the text.

••• CHECKLIST FOR INFORMATIONAL TEXT ELEMENTS

In order to identify characteristics and structural elements of informational texts, note the following:

- ✓ key details in the text that provide information about individuals, events, and ideas
- ✓ interactions between specific individuals, ideas, or events
- ✓ important developments over the course of the text
- ✓ transition words and phrases that signal interactions between individuals, events, and ideas, such as because, as a consequence, or as a result
- ✓ similarities and differences of types of information in a text

To analyze a complex set of ideas or sequence of events and explain how specific

- ✓ individuals, ideas, or events interact and develop over the course of the text, consider the following questions:
- ✓ How does the author present the information as a sequence of events?
- ✓ How does the order in which ideas or events are presented affect the connections between them?
- ✓ How do specific individuals, ideas, or events interact and develop over the course of the text?
- ✓ What other features, if any, help readers to analyze the events, ideas, or individuals in the text?

⑤ ↻ YOUR TURN

1. What does the author's use of the transition phrase "for instance" tell the reader?
   - ○ A. that the sentence includes an example to support the idea in the sentence before it
   - ○ B. that the sentence includes an example to support the idea in the sentence after it
   - ○ C. that the author's main point in the paragraph is explained in the sentence.
   - ○ D. that the second half of the paragraph discusses a new topic

2. Why does the author compare Gilbert Osmond to Tony Soprano in paragraph 5?
   - ○ A. to conclude that Soprano is a more likeable character than Osmond
   - ○ B. to show a counterexample to his thesis that he then refutes
   - ○ C. to give clear and concrete evidence to support his thesis
   - ○ D. to refer to a character in a novel that all Americans have read

6

ARE THE NEW 'GOLDEN AGE'
TV SHOWS THE NEW NOVELS?

Close Read

Reread "Are the New 'Golden Age' TV Shows the New Novels?" As you reread, complete the Skills Focus questions below. Then use your answers and annotations from the questions to help you complete the Write activity.

◎ SKILLS FOCUS

1. What are the advantages and disadvantages of how TV shows are structured? Use textual evidence to support your answer.

2. Mohsin Hamid believes that TV shows pose a real threat for novelists, and that novelists will need to find a way to adapt in the future. How does Hamid structure his argument?

3. Highlight two examples of supporting evidence in Kirsch's essay. How does the author connect these pieces of evidence to other parts of his argument?

4. Although the authors have different ideas about the role of literature in our lives, they both see a future for both novels and TV shows. What direction would each author give to these artforms? Highlight and annotate examples from the text to support your answer.

✎ WRITE

7

EXPLANATORY ESSAY: Select one of the articles. Analyze how the author uses examples, explanations, and concluding remarks to support his thesis and provide direction to his ideas. Remember to use textual evidence to support your points.

Please note that excerpts and passages in the StudySync® library and this workbook are intended as touchstones to generate interest in an author's work. The excerpts and passages do not substitute for the reading of entire texts, and StudySync strongly recommends that students seek out and purchase the whole literary or informational work in order to experience it as the author intended. Links to online resellers are available in our digital library. In addition, complete works may be ordered through an authorized reseller by filling out and returning to StudySync® the order form enclosed in this workbook.

8

Fate or
Foolishness

FICTION

Introduction

An accident creates a violent element that threatens the planet. Can a human and a computerized bird restore things to normal?

8

⒱ VOCABULARY

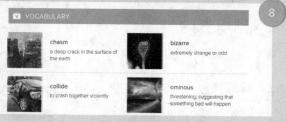

chasm
a deep crack in the surface of the earth

bizarre
extremely strange or odd

collide
to crash together violently

ominous
threatening; suggesting that something bad will happen

---

6 ## Close Read & Skills Focus

After you have completed the First Read, you will be asked to go back and read the text more closely and critically. Before you begin your Close Read, you should read through the Skills Focus to get an idea of the concepts you will want to focus on during your second reading. You should work through the Skills Focus by making annotations, highlighting important concepts, and writing notes or questions in the "Notes" column. Depending on instructions from your teacher, you may need to respond online or use a separate piece of paper to start expanding on your thoughts and ideas.

7 ## Write

Your study of each selection will end with a writing assignment. For this assignment, you should use your notes, annotations, personal ideas, and answers to both the Think and Skills Focus questions. Be sure to read the prompt carefully and address each part of it in your writing.

8 ## English Language Learner

The English Language Learner texts focus on improving language proficiency. You will practice learning strategies and skills in individual and group activities to become better readers, writers, and speakers.

Copyright © BookheadEd Learning, LLC

Extended Writing Project and Grammar

This is your opportunity to use genre characteristics and craft to compose meaningful, longer written works exploring the theme of each unit. You will draw information from your readings, research, and own life experiences to complete the assignment.

1 Writing Project

After you have read all of the unit text selections, you will move on to a writing project. Each project will guide you through the process of writing your essay. Student models will provide guidance and help you organize your thoughts. One unit ends with an **Extended Oral Project** which will give you an opportunity to develop your oral language and communication skills.

2 Writing Process Steps

There are four steps in the writing process: Plan, Draft, Revise, and Edit and Publish. During each step, you will form and shape your writing project, and each lesson's peer review will give you the chance to receive feedback from your peers and teacher.

3 Writing Skills

Each Skill lesson focuses on a specific strategy or technique that you will use during your writing project. Each lesson presents a process for applying the skill to your own work and gives you the opportunity to practice it to improve your writing.

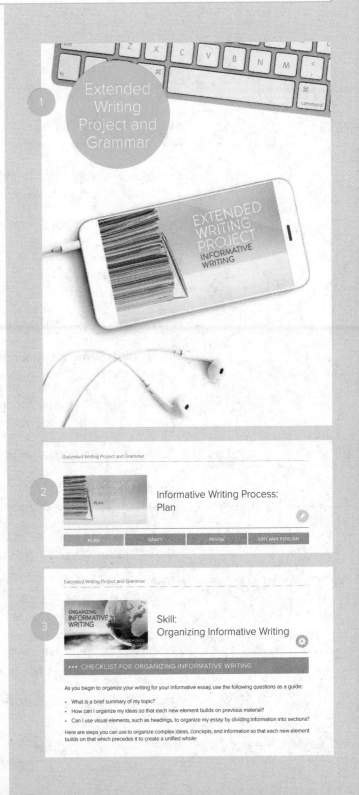

Extended Writing Project and Grammar

Informative Writing Process: Plan

| PLAN | DRAFT | REVISE | EDIT AND PUBLISH |

Extended Writing Project and Grammar

Skill: Organizing Informative Writing

••• CHECKLIST FOR ORGANIZING INFORMATIVE WRITING

As you begin to organize your writing for your informative essay, use the following questions as a guide:

• What is a brief summary of my topic?
• How can I organize my ideas so that each new element builds on previous material?
• Can I use visual elements, such as headings, to organize my essay by dividing information into sections?

Here are steps you can use to organize complex ideas, concepts, and information so that each new element builds on that which precedes it to create a unified whole:

Copyright © BookheadEd Learning, LLC

What's Next?

How can we transform the future?

Genre Focus: INFORMATIONAL

Texts

 Paired Readings

Please note that excerpts and passages in the StudySync® library and this workbook are intended as touchstones to generate interest in an author's work. The excerpts and passages do not substitute for the reading of entire texts, and StudySync® strongly recommends that students seek out and purchase the whole literary or informational work in order to experience it as the author intended. Links to online resellers are available in our digital library. In addition, complete works may be ordered through an authorized reseller by filling out and returning to StudySync® the order form enclosed in this workbook.

Copyright © BookheadEd Learning, LLC

Extended Writing Project and Grammar

English Language Learner Resources

Copyright © BookheadEd Learning, LLC

Please note that excerpts and passages in the StudySync® library and this workbook are intended as touchstones to generate interest in an author's work. The excerpts and passages do not substitute for the reading of entire texts, and StudySync® strongly recommends that students seek out and purchase the whole literary or informational work in order to experience it as the author intended. Links to online resellers are available in our digital library. In addition, complete works may be ordered through an authorized reseller by filling out and returning to StudySync® the order form enclosed in this workbook.

Unit 1: What's Next?
How can we transform the future?

CHIMAMANDA NGOZI ADICHIE

Chimamanda Ngozi Adichie (b. 1977) is a writer from Nigeria, who grew up in the house formerly owned by world-famous author Chinua Achebe. She attended college and graduate school in the United States and writes novels, short stories, and essays. In 2013, a speech Adichie gave for TEDxEuston called "We Should All Be Feminists" was sampled in the song "Flawless" by Beyoncé. In 2014, Adichie adapted the speech into a book-length essay of the same name.

FREDERICK DOUGLASS

A vital leader in the abolitionist movement, Frederick Douglass (1818–1895) was the first African American to serve as a United States official and was nominated for vice president of the United States. He was well-regarded in his time as a brilliant and eloquent speaker. Douglass's autobiographical writings, including *Narrative of the Life of Frederick Douglass, An American Slave* (1845), offer a portrait of slavery from the point of view of the enslaved, a much-needed contribution to literature that continues to be widely read.

MOHSIN HAMID

Mohsin Hamid (b. 1971) is a Pakistani American author of four novels. He drafted his first book in a college fiction workshop taught by the writer Toni Morrison, and he believes in the power of literature to visualize different and better ways to live. In an interview published in *The New Yorker,* Hamid stated, "Part of the great political crisis we face in the world today is a failure to imagine plausible desirable futures."

FRANZ KAFKA

Franz Kafka (1883–1924) was born into a middle-class, German-speaking Jewish family in Prague. He was educated as a lawyer and worked for an insurance company, writing on the side, until his death at age forty from tuberculosis. Kafka's stories often feature an isolated protagonist in a nightmarish situation, fusing realism and fantasy. Much of the work Kafka is known for was published posthumously by his friend Max Brod, who had been entrusted to burn the writer's work.

JOHN F. KENNEDY

John F. Kennedy (1917–1963) was the 35th president of the United States, whose brief time in office was colored by Cold War tensions with the Soviet Union and its allies. Shortly after Kennedy's term began in 1961, Russian cosmonaut Yuri Gagarin became the first man in space, and many Americans perceived the United States was losing the so-called space race. Kennedy declared that sending an American to the moon would allow the United States to "catch up and overtake" the Soviet Union in the unclaimed frontier of outer space.

ANNE LAMOTT

As a child growing up in San Francisco, Anne Lamott (b. 1954) was encouraged by her father, also a writer, to take a disciplined approach to the practice—to write every day, and to commit to finishing the pieces she started. By the age of twenty-six, Lamott was a published novelist and has since authored nearly twenty works of fiction and nonfiction. Her best-known book, *Bird by Bird: Some Instructions on Writing and Life* (1994), offers advice on everything from "Getting Started" to "Writer's Block" to "Finding Your Voice."

URSULA MCPIKE

Ursula McPike (b. 1961) grew up in the Detroit area and has always loved to travel. She has lived in Chicago for the last 30+ years, after first visiting the city as a girl and falling in love with the Museum of Science and Industry. She is influenced by reading about cultural differences and topics that draw debate. "Reading a book," according to McPike, "is the closest you can get to making a new friend."

DENA SIMMONS

Dena Simmons (b. 1983) grew up in the Bronx, in a one-bedroom apartment with her two sisters and her mother, who had immigrated to New York from Antigua. When she became the recipient of a scholarship to a majority white boarding school, despite her abundant qualifications, Simmons experienced the feelings of inadequacy and fraud associated with "imposter syndrome." Her career thereafter has been staked in activism and education, as she works to promote culturally responsive practices in the classroom.

ELISSA WASHUTA

Elissa Washuta (b. 1985), a member of the Cowlitz Indian tribe, grew up during a time when Hollywood put forth problematic images of indigenous characters in films like *The Last of the Mohicans* (1992), *Pocahontas* (1995), and *The Indian in the Cupboard* (1995), among others. Washuta is a writer of personal essays and memoir, and her work questions narratives of Native peoples as well as a range of contemporary issues.

MADDIE BADEN, CONNOR BALTHAZOR, GINA MATHEW, TRINA PAUL, KALI POENITSKE, AND PATRICK SULLIVAN

In 2017, high school investigative journalists Maddie Baden, Connor Balthazor, Gina Mathew, Trina Paul, Kali Poenitske, and Patrick Sullivan exposed their newly-hired principal for providing credentials from a false institution. Their story became national news, the principal resigned, and the district hired a replacement. Students at Pittsburg High School are now granted independent control over their editorial content, by the Kansas Student Publications Act, including articles that challenge or criticize the school.

ADAM KIRSCH

Adam Kirsch (b. 1979) is a Los Angeles–born poet, editor, and literary critic who started penning poems at the age of fourteen. He believes literature does not, like science or technology, advance with each new discovery. In an article for *The Atlantic*, Kirsch wrote, "Homer is just as groundbreaking today as he was 2,500 years ago." His work reveals a deep interest in the preservation of traditional literary forms, as shown in his use of meter and rhyme in his three published collections of poetry.

Are the New 'Golden Age' TV Shows the New Novels?

INFORMATIONAL TEXT
Adam Kirsch and Mohsin Hamid
2014

Introduction

studysync

Adam Kirsch (b. 1976) is a magazine editor, educator, and poet. He is also a literary critic, winning the Roger Shattuck Prize for Criticism in 2010. Mohsin Hamid (b. 1971) is a novelist, known best for *The Reluctant Fundamentalist, Exit West,* and his PEN/Hemingway Award finalist *Moth Smoke.* In this op-ed essay from the *New York Times,* both writers share their thoughts on how contemporary TV has changed how we think about the novel. Through a discussion of the style of Charles Dickens' writing, and an examination of novelistic features, both authors present persuasive arguments for their answer to the question "Are the New 'Golden Age' TV Shows the New Novels?"

To liken TV shows to novels suggests an odd ambivalence toward both genres.

By Adam Kirsch

One criticism that could be leveled against quality cable TV is that it is not nearly as formally adventurous as Dickens himself.

1   Television was so bad for so long, it's no surprise that the arrival of good television has caused the culture to lose its head a bit. Since the debut of "The Sopranos" in 1999, we have been living, so we are regularly informed, in a "golden age" of television. And over the last few years, it's become common to hear variations on the idea that quality cable TV shows are the new novels. Thomas Doherty, writing in *The Chronicle of Higher Education*, called the new genre "Arc TV"—because its stories follow long, complex arcs of development—and insisted that "at its best, the world of Arc TV is as exquisitely calibrated as the social matrix of a Henry James novel."

2   To liken TV shows to novels suggests an odd **ambivalence** toward both genres. Clearly, the comparison is intended to honor TV, by associating it with the prestige and complexity that traditionally belong to literature. But at the same time, it is covertly a form of aggression against literature, suggesting that novels have ceded their role to a younger, more popular, more dynamic art form. Mixed feelings about literature — the desire to annex its virtues while simultaneously belittling them — are typical of our culture today, which doesn't know quite how to deal with an art form, like the novel, that is both democratic and demanding.

3   It's not surprising that the novelist most often mentioned in this context is Charles Dickens. Dickens, like Shakespeare, was both a writer of genius and a popular entertainer, proving that seriousness of purpose didn't preclude accessibility. His novels appeared in serial installments, like episodes of TV shows, and teemed with minor characters, the literary equivalent of character actors. "The Wire," in particular, has been likened to a Dickens novel, for its attention to the details of poverty and class in America. Bill Moyers was echoing what has become conventional wisdom when he said that what Dickens was "to the smoky mean streets of Victorian London, David Simon is to America today."

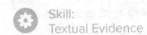
Skill:
Textual Evidence

Before 1999, television was generally lower quality than the innovative television shows after 1999. The pre-1999 shows did not follow complex story arcs throughout a season the way that a novel does from start to finish.

Copyright © BookheadEd Learning, LLC

Please note that excerpts and passages in the StudySync® library and this workbook are intended as touchstones to generate interest in an author's work. The excerpts and passages do not substitute for the reading of entire texts, and StudySync® strongly recommends that students seek out and purchase the whole literary or informational work in order to experience it as the author intended. Links to online resellers are available in our digital library. In addition, complete works may be ordered through an authorized reseller by filling out and returning to StudySync® the order form enclosed in this workbook.

NOTES

Skill:
Textual
Evidence

Dickens's episodic
storytelling is similar to
cable TV shows'
narrative structure.
For example, Dickens
was able to weave
scenes together in a
way that is similar to a
video montage of
shorter scenes put
together into a whole.

Skill:
Text-Dependent
Responses

Kirsch supports his
argument by listing
characteristics unique
to literature, such as
"voice" and "tone." He
thinks TV is still good,
but watching TV is not
the same experience as
reading literature.

4   Ironically, the comparison to Dickens, which is meant to suggest that TV has reached a new level of quality, harks back to the very beginning of modern filmmaking. Already in 1944, Sergei Eisenstein suggested in a landmark essay that the film grammar invented by D. W. Griffith was deeply indebted to Dickens's narrative strategies. Dickens, he wrote, was the real inventor of montage. If today's best TV feels Dickensian, that may be because the conventions of filmed storytelling themselves derive from Dickens — who in turn, Eisenstein points out, was influenced by the stage **melodramas** of his day. Indeed, one criticism that could be leveled against quality cable TV is that it is not nearly as formally adventurous as Dickens himself. Its visual **idiom** tends to be conventional even when its subject matter is ostentatiously provocative.

5   But comparing even the best TV shows with Dickens, or Henry James, also suggests how much the novel can achieve that TV doesn't even attempt. Televised evil, for instance, almost always takes melodramatic form: Our anti-heroes are mobsters, meth dealers or terrorists. But this has nothing to do with the way we encounter evil in real life, which is why a character like Gilbert Osmond, in "The Portrait of a Lady," is more chilling in his bullying egotism than Tony Soprano with all his stranglings and shootings.

6   Spectacle and melodrama remain at the heart of TV, as they do with all arts that must reach a large audience in order to be economically viable. But it is voice, tone, the sense of the author's mind at work, that are the essence of literature, and they exist in language, not in images. This doesn't mean we shouldn't be grateful for our good TV shows; but let's not fool ourselves into thinking that they give us what only literature can.

Copyright © BookheadEd Learning, LLC

Please note that excerpts and passages in the StudySync® library and this workbook are intended as touchstones to generate interest in an author's work. The excerpts and passages do not substitute for the reading of entire texts, and StudySync® strongly recommends that students seek out and purchase the whole literary or informational work in order to experience it as the author intended. Links to online resellers are available in our digital library. In addition, complete works may be ordered through an authorized reseller by filling out and returning to StudySync® the order form enclosed in this workbook.

The writing has improved remarkably, as have the acting, direction and design.

Copyright © BookheadEd Learning, LLC

By Mohsin Hamid

Ask novelists whether they spend more time watching TV or reading fiction and prepare yourself to hear them say the unsayable.

7 Movies have always seemed to me a much tighter form of storytelling than novels, requiring greater compression, and in that sense falling somewhere between the short story and the novel in scale. To watch a feature film is to be immersed in its world for an hour and a half, or maybe two, or exceptionally three. A novel that takes only three hours to read would be a short novel indeed, and novels that last five times as long are commonplace.

8 Television is more **capacious**. Episode after episode, and season after season, a serial drama can uncoil for dozens of hours before reaching its end. Along the way, its characters and plot have room to develop, to change course, to congeal. In its near limitlessness, TV rivals the novel.

9 What once sheltered the novel were differences in the quality of writing. Films could be well written, but they were smaller than novels. TV was big, but its writing was clunky. The novel had "Pride and Prejudice"; TV had "Dynasty." But television has made enormous leaps in the last decade or so. The writing has improved remarkably, as have the acting, direction and design.

10 Recently we've been treated to many shows that seem better than any that came before: the brilliant ethnography of "The Wire," the dazzling sci-fi of "Battlestar Galactica," the gorgeous period re-creation of "Mad Men," the gripping fantasy of "Game of Thrones," the lacerating self-exploration of "Girls." Nor is TV's rise confined to shows originating in only one country. Pakistani, Indian, British and dubbed Turkish dramas are all being devoured here in Pakistan. Thanks to downloads, even Denmark's "Borgen" has found its local niche.

11 I now watch a lot of TV. And I'm not alone, even among my colleagues. Ask novelists today whether they spend more time watching TV or reading fiction and prepare yourself, at least occasionally, to hear them say the unsayable.

Please note that excerpts and passages in the StudySync® library and this workbook are intended as touchstones to generate interest in an author's work. The excerpts and passages do not substitute for the reading of entire texts, and StudySync® strongly recommends that students seek out and purchase the whole literary or informational work in order to experience it as the author intended. Links to online resellers are available in our digital library. In addition, complete works may be ordered through an authorized reseller by filling out and returning to StudySync® the order form enclosed in this workbook.

NOTES

12 That this represents a crisis for the novel seems to me undeniable. But a crisis can be an opportunity. It **incites** change. And the novel needs to keep changing if it is to remain novel. It must, pilfering a phrase from TV, boldly go where no one has gone before.

13 In the words of the Canadian writer Sheila Heti: "Now that there are these impeccable serial dramas, writers of fiction should feel let off the hook more — not feel obliged to worry so much about plot or character, since audiences can get their fill of plot and character and story there, so novelists can take off in other directions, like what happened with painting when photography came into being more than a hundred years ago. After that there was an incredible flourishing of the art, in so many fascinating directions. The novel should only do what the serial drama could never do."

14 Television is not the new novel. Television is the old novel.

Skill:
Informational Text Elements

Hamid tells novelists to embrace the novel's "weirdness" to stay relevant "in the future." Hamid believes the novel is weird because it is intimate yet vast. TV, in contrast, is a "small world."

15 In the future, novelists need not abandon plot and character, but would do well to bear in mind the novel's weirdness. . . . Novels are characterized by their intimacy, which is extreme, by their scale, which is vast, and by their form, which is linguistic and synesthetic. . . .

16 Television gives us something that looks like a small world, made by a group of people who are themselves a small world. The novel gives us sounds pinned down by hieroglyphs, refracted flickerings inside an individual.

17 Sufis tell of two paths to transcendence: One is to look out at the universe and see yourself, the other is to look within yourself and see the universe. Their destinations may converge, but television and the novel travel in opposite directions.

From The New York Times (nytimes.com), Feb. 25, 2014 © 2014 The New York Times. All rights reserved. Used by permission and protected by the Copyright Laws of the United States. The printing, copying, redistribution, or retransmission of this Content without express written permission is prohibited.

Copyright © BookheadEd Learning, LLC

Please note that excerpts and passages in the StudySync® library and this workbook are intended as touchstones to generate interest in an author's work. The excerpts and passages do not substitute for the reading of entire texts, and StudySync® strongly recommends that students seek out and purchase the whole literary or informational work in order to experience it as the author intended. Links to online resellers are available in our digital library. In addition, complete works may be ordered through an authorized reseller by filling out and returning to StudySync® the order form enclosed in this workbook.

Skill: Text-Dependent Responses

Use the Checklist to analyze Text-Dependent Responses in "Are the New 'Golden Age' TV Shows the New Novels?" Refer to the sample student annotations about Text-Dependent Responses in the text.

••• CHECKLIST FOR TEXT-DEPENDENT RESPONSES

In order to identify strong and thorough textual evidence that supports an analysis, note the following:

✓ strong and thorough details from the text to make an inference or draw a conclusion. Inferences are sound, logical assumptions about information in a text that is not explicitly stated. To practice, you should:

- read closely and consider why an author provides or excludes particular details and information

- apply textual evidence and your own knowledge and experiences to help you figure out what the author does not state directly

- cite several pieces of textual evidence that offer strong support for your analysis

- note where textual evidence is lacking, leaving some matters uncertain

✓ strong and thorough details to support your ideas and opinions about a text

✓ explicit evidence of an author's ideas in an informational text

- explicit evidence is stated directly and must be cited accurately to support a text-dependent response

To cite strong and thorough textual evidence to support an analysis, including determining where the text leaves matters uncertain, consider the following questions:

✓ What strong and thorough textual evidence can I use to support an analysis of a text?

✓ Where does the text leave matters uncertain? How will that affect my analysis?

✓ If I infer things in the text that the author does not state directly, what evidence can I use to support my analysis?

Copyright © BookheadEd Learning, LLC

Please note that excerpts and passages in the StudySync® library and this workbook are intended as touchstones to generate interest in an author's work. The excerpts and passages do not substitute for the reading of entire texts, and StudySync® strongly recommends that students seek out and purchase the whole literary or informational work in order to experience it as the author intended. Links to online resellers are available in our digital library. In addition, complete works may be ordered through an authorized reseller by filling out and returning to StudySync® the order form enclosed in this workbook.

Reading & Writing Companion

Skill: Text-Dependent Responses

Reread paragraphs 7–11 of "Are the New 'Golden Age' TV Shows the New Novels?" Then, using the Checklist on the previous page, answer the multiple-choice questions below.

⟳ YOUR TURN

1. In paragraph 7, Hamid reveals that "Movies have always seemed to me a much tighter form of storytelling than novels, requiring greater compression, and in that sense falling somewhere between the short story and the novel in scale." Which commentary best responds to this textual evidence?

   ○ A. This textual evidence shows that storytelling in movies is more like a short story than a novel.

   ○ B. This textual evidence shows that storytelling in movies is tighter and smaller in scope than novels.

   ○ C. This textual evidence shows that storytelling in movies is similar to storytelling in television.

   ○ D. This textual evidence shows that storytelling in movies is greater in scale and larger in scope than novels.

2. Which evidence best supports the idea that television is more like a novel than a movie because there is more time to develop characters?

   ○ A. "A novel that takes only three hours to read would be a short novel indeed, and novels that last five times as long are commonplace."

   ○ B. "Episode after episode, and season after season, a serial drama can uncoil for dozens of hours before reaching its end."

   ○ C. "Films could be well written, but they were smaller than novels."

   ○ D. "Ask novelists whether they spend more time watching TV or reading fiction and prepare yourself to hear them say the unsayable."

Copyright © BookheadEd Learning, LLC

Reading & Writing Companion

Please note that excerpts and passages in the StudySync® library and this workbook are intended as touchstones to generate interest in an author's work. The excerpts and passages do not substitute for the reading of entire texts, and StudySync® strongly recommends that students seek out and purchase the whole literary or informational work in order to experience it as the author intended. Links to online resellers are available in our digital library. In addition, complete works may be ordered through an authorized reseller by filling out and returning to StudySync® the order form enclosed in this workbook.

First Read

Read "Are the New 'Golden Age' TV Shows the New Novels?" After you read, complete the Think Questions below.

☁ THINK QUESTIONS

1. What does Kirsch say about how TV has changed recently? What is the "new genre" he mentions? Use evidence from the text to support your answer.

2. Why do people often compare "good" TV to the writing of Charles Dickens? What does Kirsch say about Dickens's writing that welcomes this comparison? Use evidence from the text to support your answer.

3. What are the reasons Hamid gives for watching more television than in the past? Use evidence from the text to support your answer.

4. What is the meaning of the word **capacious** as it is used in the text? Write your best definition here, along with a brief explanation of how you inferred its meaning through context.

5. Read the following dictionary entry:

idiom

id•i•om /ˈidēəm/ *noun*

1. a group of words, that when used together, have an unclear meaning when read literally
2. a form of expression natural to a language, person, or group of people
3. the dialect of a people or part of a country
4. a characteristic mode of expression in music, literature or art

Which definition most closely matches the meaning of idiom as it is used in paragraph 4? Write the correct definition of idiom here and explain how you figured out its meaning.

Copyright © BookheadEd Learning, LLC

Please note that excerpts and passages in the StudySync® library and this workbook are intended as touchstones to generate interest in an author's work. The excerpts and passages do not substitute for the reading of entire texts, and StudySync® strongly recommends that students seek out and purchase the whole literary or informational work in order to experience it as the author intended. Links to online resellers are available in our digital library. In addition, complete works may be ordered through an authorized reseller by filling out and returning to StudySync® the order form enclosed in this workbook.

Reading & Writing Companion 7

Skill:
Textual Evidence

Use the Checklist to analyze Textual Evidence in "Are the New 'Golden Age' TV Shows the New Novels?" Refer to the sample student annotations about Textual Evidence in the text.

••• CHECKLIST FOR TEXTUAL EVIDENCE

In order to support an analysis by citing evidence that is explicitly stated in the text, do the following:

- ✓ read the text closely and critically

- ✓ identify what the text says explicitly

- ✓ find the most relevant textual evidence that supports your analysis

- ✓ consider why an author explicitly states specific details and information

- ✓ cite the specific words, phrases, sentences, or paragraphs from the text that support your analysis

- ✓ determine where evidence in the text still leaves certain matters uncertain or unresolved

In order to interpret implicit meanings in a text by making inferences, do the following:

- ✓ combine information directly stated in the text with your own knowledge, experiences, and observations

- ✓ cite the specific words, phrases, sentences, or paragraphs from the text that led to and support this inference.

Copyright © BookheadEd Learning, LLC

Please note that excerpts and passages in the StudySync® library and this workbook are intended as touchstones to generate interest in an author's work. The excerpts and passages do not substitute for the reading of entire texts, and StudySync® strongly recommends that students seek out and purchase the whole literary or informational work in order to experience it as the author intended. Links to online resellers are available in our digital library. In addition, complete works may be ordered through an authorized reseller by filling out and returning to StudySync® the order form enclosed in this workbook.

In order to cite textual evidence to support an analysis of what the text says explicitly as well as inferences drawn from the text, consider the following questions:

- ✓ Have I read the text closely and critically?

- ✓ What inferences am I making about the text?

- ✓ What textual evidence am I using to support these inferences?

- ✓ Am I quoting the evidence from the text correctly?

- ✓ Does my textual evidence logically relate to my analysis or the inference I am making?

- ✓ Does evidence in the text still leave certain matters unanswered or unresolved? In what ways?

Copyright © BookheadEd Learning, LLC

Please note that excerpts and passages in the StudySync® library and this workbook are intended as touchstones to generate interest in an author's work. The excerpts and passages do not substitute for the reading of entire texts, and StudySync® strongly recommends that students seek out and purchase the whole literary or informational work in order to experience it as the author intended. Links to online resellers are available in our digital library. In addition, complete works may be ordered through an authorized reseller by filling out and returning to StudySync® the order form enclosed in this workbook.

Reading & Writing Companion   9

Skill:
Textual Evidence

Reread paragraphs 7–9 of "Are the New 'Golden Age' TV Shows the New Novels?" Then, using the Checklist on the previous page, answer the multiple-choice questions below.

↻ YOUR TURN

1. According to the text, a novel is similar to a television series because—

   ○ A. the writing is consistently excellent for both.
   ○ B. the storytelling must be concise and compressed in both.
   ○ C. they both appeal to people who dislike watching movies.
   ○ D. they both allow for effective character and plot development.

2. In paragraph 9, which word best supports the author's claim that television used to be inferior to novels?

   ○ A. "sheltered"
   ○ B. "smaller"
   ○ C. "clunky"
   ○ D. "leaps"

Copyright © BookheadEd Learning, LLC

Please note that excerpts and passages in the StudySync® library and this workbook are intended as touchstones to generate interest in an author's work. The excerpts and passages do not substitute for the reading of entire texts, and StudySync® strongly recommends that students seek out and purchase the whole literary or informational work in order to experience it as the author intended. Links to online resellers are available in our digital library. In addition, complete works may be ordered through an authorized reseller by filling out and returning to StudySync® the order form enclosed in this workbook.

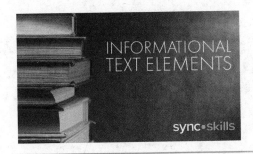

Skill: Informational Text Elements

Use the Checklist to analyze Informational Text Elements in "Are the New 'Golden Age' TV Shows the New Novels?" Refer to the sample student annotations about Informational Text Elements in the text.

••• CHECKLIST FOR INFORMATIONAL TEXT ELEMENTS

In order to identify characteristics and structural elements of informational texts, note the following:

- ✓ key details in the text that provide information about individuals, events, and ideas

- ✓ interactions between specific individuals, ideas, or events

- ✓ important developments over the course of the text

- ✓ transition words and phrases that signal interactions between individuals, events, and ideas, such as *because, as a consequence,* or *as a result*

- ✓ similarities and differences of types of information in a text

To analyze a complex set of ideas or sequence of events and explain how specific

- ✓ individuals, ideas, or events interact and develop over the course of the text, consider the following questions:

- ✓ How does the author present the information as a sequence of events?

- ✓ How does the order in which ideas or events are presented affect the connections between them?

- ✓ How do specific individuals, ideas, or events interact and develop over the course of the text?

- ✓ What other features, if any, help readers to analyze the events, ideas, or individuals in the text?

Please note that excerpts and passages in the StudySync® library and this workbook are intended as touchstones to generate interest in an author's work. The excerpts and passages do not substitute for the reading of entire texts, and StudySync® strongly recommends that students seek out and purchase the whole literary or informational work in order to experience it as the author intended. Links to online resellers are available in our digital library. In addition, complete works may be ordered through an authorized reseller by filling out and returning to StudySync® the order form enclosed in this workbook.

Copyright © BookheadEd Learning, LLC

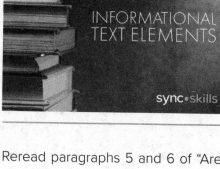

Skill: Informational Text Elements

Reread paragraphs 5 and 6 of "Are the New 'Golden Age' TV Shows the New Novels?" Then, using the Checklist on the previous page, answer the multiple-choice questions below.

⟳ YOUR TURN

1. What does the author's use of the transition phrase "for instance" tell the reader?

   ○ A. that the sentence includes an example to support the idea in the sentence before it
   ○ B. that the sentence includes an example to support the idea in the sentence after it
   ○ C. that the author's main point in the paragraph is explained in the sentence.
   ○ D. that the second half of the paragraph discusses a new topic

2. Why does the author compare Gilbert Osmond to Tony Soprano in paragraph 5?

   ○ A. to conclude that Soprano is a more likeable character than Osmond
   ○ B. to show a counterexample to his thesis that he then refutes
   ○ C. to give clear and concrete evidence to support his thesis
   ○ D. to refer to a character in a novel that all Americans have read

Copyright © BookheadEd Learning, LLC

Please note that excerpts and passages in the StudySync® library and this workbook are intended as touchstones to generate interest in an author's work. The excerpts and passages do not substitute for the reading of entire texts, and StudySync® strongly recommends that students seek out and purchase the whole literary or informational work in order to experience it as the author intended. Links to online resellers are available in our digital library. In addition, complete works may be ordered through an authorized reseller by filling out and returning to StudySync® the order form enclosed in this workbook.

Close Read

Reread "Are the New 'Golden Age' TV Shows the New Novels?" As you reread, complete the Skills Focus questions below. Then use your answers and annotations from the questions to help you complete the Write activity.

◎ SKILLS FOCUS

1. What are the advantages and disadvantages of how TV shows are structured? Use textual evidence to support your answer.

2. Mohsin Hamid believes that TV shows pose a real threat for novelists, and that novelists will need to find a way to adapt in the future. How does Hamid structure his argument?

3. Highlight two examples of supporting evidence in Kirsch's essay. How does the author connect these pieces of evidence to other parts of his argument?

4. Although the authors have different ideas about the role of literature in our lives, they both see a future for both novels and TV shows. What direction would each author give to these artforms? Highlight and annotate examples from the text to support your answer.

✏ WRITE

EXPLANATORY ESSAY: Select one of the articles. Analyze how the author uses examples, explanations, and concluding remarks to support his thesis and provide direction to his ideas. Remember to use textual evidence to support your points.

Copyright © BookheadEd Learning, LLC

Please note that excerpts and passages in the StudySync® library and this workbook are intended as touchstones to generate interest in an author's work. The excerpts and passages do not substitute for the reading of entire texts, and StudySync® strongly recommends that students seek out and purchase the whole literary or informational work in order to experience it as the author intended. Links to online resellers are available in our digital library. In addition, complete works may be ordered through an authorized reseller by filling out and returning to StudySync® the order form enclosed in this workbook.

Reading & Writing Companion   13

Community Colleges vs. Technical Schools

INFORMATIONAL TEXT
Ursula McPike
2018

Introduction

Before students begin the college application process, it is important that they are aware of the options available to them. This text offers key information and comparisons between what one will find at a community college and what one will find at a technical school. While both provide strong educational foundations, the curricula, cost, duration, and outcomes offered differ between these institutions. "Community Colleges vs. Technical Schools" encourages students to consider these and other factors when deciding where to get an education.

"If you do some research on two-year schools, you might find one that is just right for you."

Community Colleges vs. Technical Schools

1   If you or your bank account has decided that enrolling in a four-year college is not for you, don't despair. You still have options. One choice is a community college, also called a junior college. Another choice is a technical school, also called a **vocational** or trade school. These schools offer programs that take two years or less to complete, and they serve a surprising number of students. According to the National Center for Educational Statistics, 6.1 million undergraduates (36%) were enrolled in two-year colleges in Fall 2016. To compare, 10.8 million (64%) were enrolled in four-year colleges. If you do some research on two-year schools, you might find one that is just right for you.

Community Colleges

2   A community college is a two-year government-supported college that offers an associate's degree and draws its students from a particular community. It usually offers general academic courses in English, writing, and math. It may also provide **technical** training for a specific job, such as emergency medical technician (EMT) or paralegal.

3   Admission at a community college is non-selective, meaning it is much easier to get admitted there than at a four-year college. Additionally, tuition costs at a community college are much lower than those at an in-state four year institution—typically less than half as much. Often people go to community colleges with the intention of transferring to a four-year college once they receive their associate's degree, ultimately achieving a four-year degree for much less than the typical student. Students who don't intend to transfer look forward to starting their careers (and cashing their paychecks) sooner than graduates of four-year colleges.

Things to Consider About Community Colleges

4   Although community colleges offer many benefits, some aspects of these schools need to be considered carefully. With the right financial aid package,

Copyright © BookheadEd Learning, LLC

Please note that excerpts and passages in the StudySync® library and this workbook are intended as touchstones to generate interest in an author's work. The excerpts and passages do not substitute for the reading of entire texts, and StudySync® strongly recommends that students seek out and purchase the whole literary or informational work in order to experience it as the author intended. Links to online resellers are available in our digital library. In addition, complete works may be ordered through an authorized reseller by filling out and returning to StudySync® the order form enclosed in this workbook.

Reading & Writing Companion   15

NOTES

the cost of a four-year college can be brought down to the cost of a community college. With their flexible hours and lack of student housing, community colleges were designed for working students and do not offer the athletic programs and rich social life that a four-year college does.

5   There is also a stigma, or bad perception, attached to community colleges, with many people believing that their students and teachers are less intelligent than those at four-year "regular" colleges. Secondly, although community college students start working sooner, students from traditional colleges eventually catch up with them in earnings. And if students plan to move on to a four-year institution, not all credits may transfer. It usually takes a transfer student an extra (fifth) year to **obtain** a bachelor's degree. Even if credits do transfer, it is is still difficult to get a degree from a four-year school after starting out at a community college. The educational research firm EAB found that out of 100 applicants to a two-year college, only nine completed their associate's degree, and only seven eventually gained a bachelor's degree from a four-year school.

Technical Colleges

6   A technical college is career-focused, giving hands-on training to students in fields such as cosmetology, culinary arts, and skilled trades such as welding. Their programs usually last two years or less. Such schools are usually private and for-profit. Their costs vary widely, but the average cost is about $33,000. Many technical school students learn their jobs through apprenticeships, where they work under an expert in their field. Technical school students find work very quickly, since there is a labor shortage of skilled workers. For the same reason, technical school students also have more job security once they begin working. Moreover, many careers in technical fields are high-paying; for instance, the U.S. Bureau of Labor Statistics reports that the median salary for an air traffic controller is $124,540, and the median salary for a dental hygienist is $74,070.

Things to Consider About Technical Colleges

7   Unlike community colleges, which offer a wide variety of courses and room to change and explore, trade schools won't let you have a do-over. If you began a nursing program and then decided you wanted to be a lab technician, you would have to start all over again. You should also keep in mind that preferred skills and school standings change rapidly. A program considered the best in one year may not be considered the best in the next year. A skill that is in high demand at one time may not be desirable later (think typewriter repair or an outdated programming language).

Copyright © BookheadEd Learning, LLC

Please note that excerpts and passages in the StudySync® library and this workbook are intended as touchstones to generate interest in an author's work. The excerpts and passages do not substitute for the reading of entire texts, and StudySync® strongly recommends that students seek out and purchase the whole literary or informational work in order to experience it as the author intended. Links to online resellers are available in our digital library. In addition, complete works may be ordered through an authorized reseller by filling out and returning to StudySync® the order form enclosed in this workbook.

NOTES

8   Although technical school graduates, like community college graduates, can start their careers sooner than four-year graduates and with less debt, the four-year graduate eventually catches up to and surpasses them in earnings. Statistics about earnings also hide that most high-paying vocational jobs are held by men, whereas women cluster in low-paying jobs such as nursing aides.

9   Keep in mind that there is a stigma against technical schools, as there is against community colleges. Many people today still hold the same attitudes about graduates from vocational schools that early 20th-century thinker John Dewey expressed:

> "[Vocational training] fits them to become cogs in the industrial machine. Free men need liberal education to make a good use of their freedom."

10   Maybe, maybe not. Distaste for vocational and community colleges can be seen as ironic now, as graduates of two-year colleges do some of the most necessary work in a community—drawing blood, repairing computers, operating water treatment plants, and countless other tasks that keep us all alive and well.

11   Furthermore, a focus on technical education can revive a community. Walla Walla Community College, faced with a decline in local industries such as agriculture, food processing, and lumber, and a rise in the numbers of workers needing to be retrained, **expanded** the number of programs it offered. It created more than 100 programs, with 60% in technical areas. One popular program was in enology and viticulture (winemaking). Over time, the number of wineries in the area grew from 16 to 200 and the hospitality sector ballooned. Hundreds of thousands of wine tourists visited, and hotels and restaurants sprang up to **accommodate** them. The town regained prosperity, due in (large) part to its additional technical education offerings.

Which type of college is better for you?

12   Take this quiz to find out. Check the box under the answer that best fits you. Most "Yes" answers indicate that a community college would be a better choice for you. Most "No" answers indicate that a technical college would be more suitable.

Yes	No	
_____	_____	Are you unsure of the exact job you desire?
_____	_____	Do you require a low tuition?

Please note that excerpts and passages in the StudySync® library and this workbook are intended as touchstones to generate interest in an author's work. The excerpts and passages do not substitute for the reading of entire texts, and StudySync® strongly recommends that students seek out and purchase the whole literary or informational work in order to experience it as the author intended. Links to online resellers are available in our digital library. In addition, complete works may be ordered through an authorized reseller by filling out and returning to StudySync® the order form enclosed in this workbook.

Copyright © BookheadEd Learning, LLC

NOTES

Yes	No	
_____	_____	Do you plan to transfer to a four-year school?
_____	_____	Can you take an extra (fifth) year to get a four-year degree?
_____	_____	Do you have somewhere to live for the time you are in school?
_____	_____	Will your credits transfer to your chosen four-year school?
_____	_____	Do you want to get a job as soon as possible?
_____	_____	Would you like knowing you have contributed to your local economy?
_____	_____	Would you prefer general academic classes over an apprenticeship?

✏ WRITE

PERSONAL RESPONSE: Write a journal entry in which you weigh your options after high school. Consider your hopes for the future as well as the resources and supports that will be available to you. Which experiences would best prepare you for your career, or perhaps help inform your decision? What might your next steps be?

Copyright © BookheadEd Learning, LLC

Please note that excerpts and passages in the StudySync® library and this workbook are intended as touchstones to generate interest in an author's work. The excerpts and passages do not substitute for the reading of entire texts, and StudySync® strongly recommends that students seek out and purchase the whole literary or informational work in order to experience it as the author intended. Links to online resellers are available in our digital library. In addition, complete works may be ordered through an authorized reseller by filling out and returning to StudySync® the order form enclosed in this workbook.

Overcoming Impostor Syndrome

INFORMATIONAL TEXT
Dena Simmons
2018

Introduction

Impostor syndrome is not a mental illness. It is a common set of negative behavioral responses to achievement. When individuals don't give themselves credit for their successes—internalizing their failures instead—they may come to see success as undeserved, or just a stroke of luck. To doubt oneself is human. But to constantly filter one's experiences so that the bad is earned and the good is undeserved is what doctors and psychologists call "impostor syndrome." Impostor syndrome is estimated to affect three out of every four people at some point in their lives. But is there hope for those that suffer from it? Author Dena Simmons reviews the syndrome

"If you struggle with impostor experiences, you are not alone."

NOTES

Skill:
Informational Text
Structure

Using headings to structure the text into categories, the author tells readers how to overcome impostor syndrome. This helps readers understand what impostor syndrome is before determining if they are affected by it.

What is impostor syndrome?

1   Do you ever sit in class and say to yourself, "I'm not smart enough to be here"? Do you ever feel like your accomplishments are mere luck, or that you simply do not deserve them? Do you back down from challenges because you fear being evaluated? If you answered "yes" to any of these questions, it is likely that you have impostor syndrome.

2   Now, you might be thinking, "What is impostor syndrome?" Well, impostor syndrome—first described in a 1978 academic paper by Dr. Pauline Clance and her colleague, Dr. Suzanne Imes—is characterized by intense feelings that make you believe that you are inadequate or a fraud, even if your accomplishments prove otherwise. Essentially, people with impostor syndrome do not **internalize** their success. Impostor syndrome goes by numerous names: impostor phenomenon, impostorism, impostor feelings, impostor experiences, impostor fears, and perceived fraudulence. Though there are slight distinctions to these constructs, the common element is having the internal experience of incompetence and fraudulence specifically related to achievement situations like school and the workplace (Sakulkum and Alexander 2011; Harvey 1985).

3   In sum, based on a 2011 article in the *International Journal of Behavioral Science* that reviewed the definitions and characteristics of impostorism (Sakulkum and Alexander 2011), people with impostor syndrome:

*   feel like a fraud and believe that others think more favorably of their successes and achievements than they do.

*   fear that other people will discover that they are a fraud and believe that they are a failure just as they believe themselves to be.

*   have difficulty internalizing their successes, and as a result, attribute their achievements to external factors.

Copyright © BookheadEd Learning, LLC

Please note that excerpts and passages in the StudySync® library and this workbook are intended as touchstones to generate interest in an author's work. The excerpts and passages do not substitute for the reading of entire texts, and StudySync® strongly recommends that students seek out and purchase the whole literary or informational work in order to experience it as the author intended. Links to online resellers are available in our digital library. In addition, complete works may be ordered through an authorized reseller by filling out and returning to StudySync® the order form enclosed in this workbook.

What impostor syndrome is not

4   People generally assume that impostor syndrome is a mental health disorder because of the use of the word *syndrome*. However, it is not a mental illness. In fact, impostor syndrome is not listed in the *Diagnostic and Statistical Manual of Mental Disorders*, which is the main authority on psychiatric **diagnoses** published by the American Psychiatric Association. However, impostor syndrome can interfere with your psychological well-being and lead to depression (Henning, Ey, and Shaw 1998) and low self-esteem (Sonnak and Towell 2001). Some people with impostor syndrome might also engage in maladaptive behaviors—behaviors that get in the way of a person's ability to function well in everyday activities, such as procrastination or over-working.

Who struggles with impostor feelings?

 Skill: Central or Main Idea

5   When impostor syndrome was first studied in 1978, researchers Drs. Clance and Imes believed that it was a phenomenon that only high-achieving women experienced. However, over the years, numerous studies have found that both men and women (Langford 1990) and people across different cultures (Clance et al. 1995) and occupations (Fried-Buchalter 1992; Topping 1983; Prata and Gietzen 2007) admit to feeling like an impostor at some point in their lives. Essentially, as discussed in a 1981 academic paper by Dr. Harvey, anyone can identify as an impostor as long as they fail to internalize their success. Dr. Harvey (1981) also found that impostor syndrome is not limited to highly successful people.

This seems like a central idea because it answers the question in the sub-heading. It also relates to defining impostor syndrome, which the previous paragraphs also do. This shows how various main ideas can build on one another.

6   In fact, if you struggle with impostor experiences, you are not alone. According to a 1985 paper by Dr. Gail Matthew and Dr. Clance, about 70% of the sample expressed having impostor feelings at some point in their lives. In addition, notable, successful people have admitted to experiencing impostorism including author Maya Angelou, technology leader Sheryl Sandberg, and actor Tom Hanks. Though diverse groups of people have struggled with impostorism, people from marginalized backgrounds tend to experience it more. This can be a result of **discrimination**, stereotype threat, or microaggressions[1] that potentially lead marginalized groups to internalize feelings of fraudulence and not belonging.

What emotions are common for people who have impostor syndrome?

7   Two emotions that people with impostor syndrome commonly feel are anxiety and fear (Clance 1985). When people feel anxious, they feel uncertain about the future. Anxiety can manifest in tension in the body, an increased heartbeat, an inability to stay still and focus, and hurried speech. People with impostor

---

1. **microaggressions** commonplace verbal or physical slights or insults that communicate a prejudice toward a marginalized group

Please note that excerpts and passages in the StudySync® library and this workbook are intended as touchstones to generate interest in an author's work. The excerpts and passages do not substitute for the reading of entire texts, and StudySync® strongly recommends that students seek out and purchase the whole literary or informational work in order to experience it as the author intended. Links to online resellers are available in our digital library. In addition, complete works may be ordered through an authorized reseller by filling out and returning to StudySync® the order form enclosed in this workbook.

Copyright © BookheadEd Learning, LLC

syndrome experience anxiety because they are not sure what will happen when and if someone finds out that they are a fraud. On the other hand, when people are fearful, they feel there is impending danger. Fear can result in tense bodies, sweaty palms, an increased heartbeat, and wide eyes. People who suffer from impostorism might be fearful about what will happen if they fail or are evaluated poorly. Will they get kicked out of a program or class? Will they be bullied? Will they be embarrassed in front of others? People with impostor syndrome also tend to experience self-doubt, shame, and frustration.

What can we do to overcome our impostor feelings?

1. Talk to others.

Skill:
Informational Text Structure

Subheadings and clearly labeled steps are effective in helping readers follow the author's instructions, which fulfills the author's purpose for writing: to teach readers how to identify and combat impostor syndrome.

8　When you share your impostor experiences with others, you realize you are not the only one struggling through it. Learning that you are not alone and that other people experience self-doubt as well as impostor feelings can be liberating. In the process of sharing impostor experiences with others, you build community and a safe space. You also begin to believe your successes and achievements are well-deserved.

How to begin:

- With friends that you trust, start a conversation where you share your own experiences of feeling like a fraud and impostor, and invite others to share theirs

- Then, together with your friends, discuss what strategies others have used to tackle their challenges and come up with a way to support each other.

Skill:
Central or Main Idea

The main idea here involves coping with impostor syndrome. The strategy interacts with the idea that anyone can experience impostor syndrome, so speaking about it should be natural and will help you realize you are not alone.

2. Engage in positive self-talk.

9　People with impostor syndrome generally engage in negative self-talk, the mean and discouraging comments they say to themselves. Some examples of negative self-talk include: "I'm not smart enough to get into my first-choice college!" or "They only accepted me because they felt bad for me." To begin to confront impostor experiences, people need to be kinder to themselves by engaging in positive self-talk, which involves saying encouraging and uplifting statements to yourself. Some examples of positive self-talk include: "You worked hard, and you earned your accomplishments!" and "You are smart enough to be in this class!" By engaging in positive self-talk, you unlock optimism and self-confidence.

How to begin:

- Make a list of the negative comments that you say to yourself often.

- Then, next to each negative comment, write a positive message to yourself instead.

- Afterwards, devise a plan to interrupt your negative self-talk with positive self-talk.

Copyright © BookheadEd Learning, LLC

Please note that excerpts and passages in the StudySync® library and this workbook are intended as touchstones to generate interest in an author's work. The excerpts and passages do not substitute for the reading of entire texts, and StudySync® strongly recommends that students seek out and purchase the whole literary or informational work in order to experience it as the author intended. Links to online resellers are available in our digital library. In addition, complete works may be ordered through an authorized reseller by filling out and returning to StudySync® the order form enclosed in this workbook.

NOTES

3. Build an emotion management strategy tool box.

10 People who have impostor syndrome tend to feel anxious, frustrated, ashamed, and fearful. These emotions feel unpleasant and can distract people from achieving their goals. That's why it is important to develop strategies to manage emotions, especially the uncomfortable emotions that come with impostorism. To manage emotions effectively, it is important to have a toolbox of strategies from which you can choose.

Emotion management strategies include:
1. Action strategies. These are ways you use your body to regulate emotions, like seeking social support, going for a run, or taking a deep breath.
2. Thought strategies. These are ways you use your mind to regulate emotions, like **visualizing** a successful outcome or reframing everything you do as a learning experience.

How to begin:
*   Write a list of thought and action strategies that you already use to manage uncomfortable emotions.
*   Put an asterisk next to those strategies that you can employ whenever you are beginning to feel like an impostor in any situation or environment.

4. Leverage your strengths to tackle the areas where you feel like an impostor.

11 Undoubtedly, you are great at something. To begin to confront your impostor feelings, it is helpful to think about your strengths as a way to build the confidence needed to tackle those areas that make you feel like an impostor.

How to begin:
*   Make a list of all of your strengths. Then, next to each strength, write down what steps you took to get good at that specific skill or activity.
*   Afterwards, write a list of the goals you want to accomplish with an action plan, leveraging some of the steps you took to develop your strengths.

5. Be self-compassionate.

12 Clance (1985) found that people who experience impostor syndrome tend to aim for perfectionism. As such, when things do not go as planned, people who struggle with impostorism feel overwhelmed or disappointed and tend to generalize their inability to meet their perfectionistic goals as evidence that they are a failure. Instead of focusing on being perfect, it is helpful to

Copyright © BookheadEd Learning, LLC

Please note that excerpts and passages in the StudySync® library and this workbook are intended as touchstones to generate interest in an author's work. The excerpts and passages do not substitute for the reading of entire texts, and StudySync® strongly recommends that students seek out and purchase the whole literary or informational work in order to experience it as the author intended. Links to online resellers are available in our digital library. In addition, complete works may be ordered through an authorized reseller by filling out and returning to StudySync® the order form enclosed in this workbook.

Reading & Writing
Companion

23

NOTES

remind yourself that everyone is entitled to make mistakes—even you. And, when you do well, do something amazing for yourself.

How to begin:

- When working on an assignment or another task, evaluate your goals by asking yourself the following questions:

  > Can I accomplish this by the deadline if there is a deadline? If you cannot, consider making changes to have a more realistic goal.

  > Will I enjoy myself while doing this task or am I just doing it to stand out among my peers? If you are not enjoying yourself, it is best you consider coming up with a goal that both challenges you accordingly and brings you joy.

  > Do I have the resources to complete the task at hand? If you do not have the resources, either create a plan to attain them or consider another task that you can complete with the resources that you have.

13 These are just some of the ways that you can begin to confront your inner impostor. You might find your own ways to manage your impostor syndrome, but whatever you do, the goal is to develop strategies to promote your personal growth, **enhance** your wellbeing, build positive relationships, and contribute to your desired goals.

References:

Clance, Pauline Rose, and Suzanne Ament Imes. "The Imposter Phenomenon in High Achieving Women: Dynamics and Therapeutic Intervention." *Psychotherapy: Theory, Research & Practice,* vol. 15, no. 3, 1978, pp. 241–247.

Clance, Pauline Rose. *The Imposter Phenomenon: Overcoming the Fear That Haunts Your Success.* Peach Tree Pub Ltd., 1985.

Clance, Pauline Rose, et al. "Imposter Phenomenon in an Interpersonal/Social Context." *Women & Therapy,* vol. 16, no. 4, 1995, pp. 79–96.

Fried-Buchalter, Sharon. "Fear of Success, Fear of Failure, and the Impostor Phenomenon Among Male and Female Marketing Managers."ikm *Sex Roles,* vol. 37, no. 11, 1997, pp. 847–859.

Harvey, J. C. *The Impostor Phenomenon and Achievement: A Failure to Internalize Success.* Dissertation, Temple University, 1981. UMI, 42. ATT 4969B.

Copyright © BookheadEd Learning, LLC

Please note that excerpts and passages in the StudySync® library and this workbook are intended as touchstones to generate interest in an author's work. The excerpts and passages do not substitute for the reading of entire texts, and StudySync® strongly recommends that students seek out and purchase the whole literary or informational work in order to experience it as the author intended. Links to online resellers are available in our digital library. In addition, complete works may be ordered through an authorized reseller by filling out and returning to StudySync® the order form enclosed in this workbook.

Kolligian, John, and Robert J. Sternberg. "Perceived Fraudulence in Young Adults: Is there an "Impostor Syndrome"?" *Journal of Personality Assessment,* vol. 56, no. 2, 1991, pp. 308–326.

Langford, Joe. *The Need to Look Smart: The Impostor Phenomenon and Motivations for Learning.* Dissertation, Georgia State University, 1990. UMI, 51. ATT 3604B.

Leary, Mark R., et al."The Impostor Phenomenon: Self-Perceptions, Reflected Appraisals, and Interpersonal Strategies." *Journal of Personality,* vol. 68, no. 4, 2000, pp. 725–756.

Matthews, Gail, and Pauline Rose Clance. "Treatment of the Impostor Phenomenon in Psychotherapy Clients." *Psychotherapy in Private Practice,* vol. 3, no. 1, 1985, pp. 71–81.

Prata, John, and Jonathan W. Gietzen. "The Imposter Phenomenon in Physician Assistant Graduates." *The Journal of Physician Assistant Education,* vol. 18, no. 4, 2007, pp. 33–36.

Sakulkum, Jaruwan, and James Alexander. "The Impostor Phenomenon." *International Journal of Behavioral Science,* vol. 6, no. 1, 2011, pp. 75–97.

Sonnak, Carina, and Tony Towell. "The Impostor Phenomenon in British University Students: Relationships Between Self-Esteem, Mental Health, Parental Rearing Style and Socioeconomic Status." *Personality and Individual Differences*, vol. 31, no. 6, 2001, pp. 863–874.

Topping, Mary Elaine Harvey. *The Impostor Phenomenon: A Study of its Construct and Incidence in University Faculty Members*. Doctoral Dissertation, University of South Florida, 1983. UMI, 44. ATT 1948B–1949B.

Dena Simmons, Ed.D., is an activist, educator, and student of life from the Bronx, New York. She serves as the Assistant Director of the Yale Center for Emotional Intelligence. She writes and speaks nationally about social justice and culturally responsive and sustaining pedagogy, as well as creating emotionally intelligent and safe classrooms within the context of equity.

Copyright © BookheadEd Learning, LLC

Please note that excerpts and passages in the StudySync® library and this workbook are intended as touchstones to generate interest in an author's work. The excerpts and passages do not substitute for the reading of entire texts, and StudySync® strongly recommends that students seek out and purchase the whole literary or informational work in order to experience it as the author intended. Links to online resellers are available in our digital library. In addition, complete works may be ordered through an authorized reseller by filling out and returning to StudySync® the order form enclosed in this workbook.

First Read

Read "Overcoming Impostor Syndrome." After you read, complete the Think Questions below.

☁ THINK QUESTIONS

1. According to the author, what is "maladaptive behavior" and how does it impact an individual? What are some other maladaptive behaviors besides the ones provided in the text? Refer to the text to support your thinking.

2. In what ways might a person with impostor syndrome worry about the future? Support your answer with examples from the text.

3. What kinds of words or actions would be helpful to a friend who is dealing with impostor syndrome? Why and how would these words or actions help? Use the text to support your answer.

4. What is the meaning of the word **diagnoses** as it is used in the text? Write your best definition here, along with a brief explanation of how you arrived at its meaning.

5. Use context clues to figure out the definition of the word **enhance** as it is used in this text. Write your definition here, then check a dictionary to confirm your understanding.

Copyright © BookheadEd Learning, LLC

Please note that excerpts and passages in the StudySync® library and this workbook are intended as touchstones to generate interest in an author's work. The excerpts and passages do not substitute for the reading of entire texts, and StudySync® strongly recommends that students seek out and purchase the whole literary or informational work in order to experience it as the author intended. Links to online resellers are available in our digital library. In addition, complete works may be ordered through an authorized reseller by filling out and returning to StudySync® the order form enclosed in this workbook.

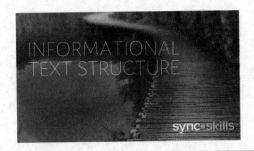

Skill: Informational Text Structure

Use the Checklist to analyze Informational Text Structure in "Overcoming Impostor Syndrome." Refer to the sample student annotations about Informational Text Structure in the text.

••• CHECKLIST FOR INFORMATIONAL TEXT STRUCTURE

In order to determine the structure an author uses in his or her exposition or argument, note the following:

✓ where the author introduces and clarifies their argument

✓ sentences and paragraphs that reveal the text structure the author uses to frame the argument

✓ whether the text structure is effective in presenting all sides of the argument, and makes his or her points clear, convincing and engaging

To analyze and evaluate the effectiveness of the structure an author uses in his or her exposition or argument, including whether the structure makes points clear, convincing, and engaging, consider the following questions:

✓ Did I have to read a particular sentence or phrase over again? Where?

✓ Did I find myself distracted or uninterested while reading the text? When?

✓ Did the structure the author used make their points clear, convincing, and engaging? Why or why not?

✓ Was the author's exposition or argument effective? Why or why not?

Copyright © BookheadEd Learning, LLC

Please note that excerpts and passages in the StudySync® library and this workbook are intended as touchstones to generate interest in an author's work. The excerpts and passages do not substitute for the reading of entire texts, and StudySync® strongly recommends that students seek out and purchase the whole literary or informational work in order to experience it as the author intended. Links to online resellers are available in our digital library. In addition, complete works may be ordered through an authorized reseller by filling out and returning to StudySync® the order form enclosed in this workbook.

Reading & Writing Companion   27

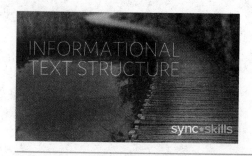

Skill: Informational Text Structure

Reread paragraph 12 of "Overcoming Impostor Syndrome." Then, using the Checklist on the previous page, answer the multiple-choice questions below.

⟳ YOUR TURN

1. Which statement best relates the author's text structure to her purpose in this excerpt?

   ○ A. The author classifies people according to whether or not they have impostor syndrome to present information about unpleasant emotions.

   ○ B. The author structures the text by dividing it into describing the problem then explaining solutions to the problem.

   ○ C. The author structures the text by explaining the advantages and disadvantages of emotion management strategies.

   ○ D. The author structures the text by comparing and contrasting people who are not affected by impostor syndrome with people who are.

2. Does the author effectively use text structure to achieve her purpose in this excerpt?

   ○ A. Yes, because the author explains how people who have impostor syndrome tend to feel anxious and ashamed.

   ○ B. Yes, because the author uses subheadings and gives organized lists of both examples and ways to begin using the strategies.

   ○ C. No, because the author should have written the entire excerpt in bulleted format, instead of alternating lists with prose.

   ○ D. No, because the author does not provide ways of using these emotional management strategies.

Copyright © BookheadEd Learning, LLC

Please note that excerpts and passages in the StudySync® library and this workbook are intended as touchstones to generate interest in an author's work. The excerpts and passages do not substitute for the reading of entire texts, and StudySync® strongly recommends that students seek out and purchase the whole literary or informational work in order to experience it as the author intended. Links to online resellers are available in our digital library. In addition, complete works may be ordered through an authorized reseller by filling out and returning to StudySync® the order form enclosed in this workbook.

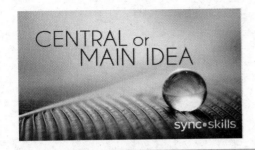

Skill: Central or Main Idea

Use the Checklist to analyze Central or Main Idea in "Overcoming Impostor Syndrome." Refer to the sample student annotations about Central or Main Idea in the text.

••• CHECKLIST FOR CENTRAL OR MAIN IDEA

In order to identify two or more central ideas of a text, note the following:

- ✓ the main idea in each paragraph or group of paragraphs

- ✓ key details in each paragraph or section of text, noticing what they have in common

- ✓ whether the details contain information that could indicate more than one main idea in a text

  - a science text, for example, may provide information about a specific environment and also a message on ecological awareness

  - a biography may contain equally important ideas about a person's achievements, influence, and the time period in which the person lives or lived

- ✓ when each central idea emerges

- ✓ ways that the central ideas interact and build on one another

To determine two or more central ideas of a text and analyze their development over the course of the text, including how they interact and build on one another to provide a complex analysis, consider the following questions:

- ✓ What main idea(s) do the details in each paragraphs explain or describe?

- ✓ What central or main ideas do all the paragraphs support?

- ✓ How do the central ideas interact and build on one another? How does that affect when they emerge?

- ✓ How might you provide an objective summary of the text? What details would you include?

Copyright © BookheadEd Learning, LLC

Please note that excerpts and passages in the StudySync® library and this workbook are intended as touchstones to generate interest in an author's work. The excerpts and passages do not substitute for the reading of entire texts, and StudySync® strongly recommends that students seek out and purchase the whole literary or informational work in order to experience it as the author intended. Links to online resellers are available in our digital library. In addition, complete works may be ordered through an authorized reseller by filling out and returning to StudySync® the order form enclosed in this workbook.

Reading & Writing Companion   29

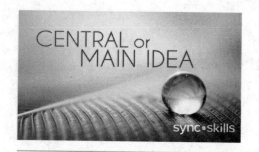

Skill: Central or Main Idea

Reread paragraph 4 of "Overcoming Impostor Syndrome." Then, using the Checklist on the previous page, answer the multiple-choice questions below.

↻ YOUR TURN

1. This question has two parts. First, answer Part A. Then, answer Part B.

   Part A: Which sentence or phrase from the excerpt best expresses the main idea of this section of the article?

   ○ A. "impostor syndrome is a mental health disorder"

   ○ B. "[impostor syndrome] is not a mental illness"

   ○ C. "impostor syndrome can interfere with your psychological well-being"

   ○ D. "Some people with impostor syndrome might also engage in maladaptive behaviors"

   Part B: How does referring to the American Psychiatric Association support the main idea that you identified in Part A?

   ○ A. The writer assumes that most readers will not be familiar with this professional organization.

   ○ B. The writer assumes that most readers will be familiar with this professional organization.

   ○ C. Citing a professional organization weakens the writer's assertion that impostor syndrome is not a mental disorder.

   ○ D. "Citing a professional organization strengthens the writer's assertion that impostor syndrome is not a mental disorder.

Copyright © BookheadEd Learning, LLC

Please note that excerpts and passages in the StudySync® library and this workbook are intended as touchstones to generate interest in an author's work. The excerpts and passages do not substitute for the reading of entire texts, and StudySync® strongly recommends that students seek out and purchase the whole literary or informational work in order to experience it as the author intended. Links to online resellers are available in our digital library. In addition, complete works may be ordered through an authorized reseller by filling out and returning to StudySync® the order form enclosed in this workbook.

Skill: Compare and Contrast

Use the Checklist to analyze Compare and Contrast in "Overcoming Impostor Syndrome." Refer to the sample student annotations about Compare and Contrast in the text.

••• CHECKLIST FOR COMPARE AND CONTRAST

In order to determine how to compare and contrast informational articles, use the following steps:

- ✓ first, choose two or more articles from reputable sources

- ✓ next, identify the main idea in each article

- ✓ after, identify the theme and purpose presented in each article

- ✓ then, identify the rhetorical features in each article, and the use of figures of speech and other compositional techniques that are designed to have a persuasive or impressive effect on readers

- ✓ finally, explain the similarities and differences between two or more of these articles, including their use of rhetoric, the themes each article explores, and their purposes.

To analyze informational articles, consider the following questions:

- ✓ Are the articles from reputable sources or written by reputable individuals?

- ✓ What themes or topics are apparent in each of these articles?

- ✓ What is the purpose of each article?

- ✓ Are there any rhetorical features in these articles? In what ways are these features similar and different?

- ✓ How are the themes, topics, and purpose in these articles similar and different?

Copyright © BookheadEd Learning, LLC

Please note that excerpts and passages in the StudySync® library and this workbook are intended as touchstones to generate interest in an author's work. The excerpts and passages do not substitute for the reading of entire texts, and StudySync® strongly recommends that students seek out and purchase the whole literary or informational work in order to experience it as the author intended. Links to online resellers are available in our digital library. In addition, complete works may be ordered through an authorized reseller by filling out and returning to StudySync® the order form enclosed in this workbook.

Skill: Compare and Contrast

Reread paragraph 13 of "Overcoming Impostor Syndrome" and paragraph 12 of "Community Colleges vs. Technical Schools." Then, using the Checklist on the previous page, answer the multiple-choice questions below.

⟳ YOUR TURN

1. Compare the conclusions from each essay. How are these two conclusions similar?

   ○ A. Both conclusions suggest there is one best way to approach these topics.
   ○ B. Both conclusions suggest that readers need to answer yes/no questions.
   ○ C. Both conclusions focus on getting readers to seek professional help.
   ○ D. Both conclusions focus on getting readers to find their own answers.

2. Contrast the conclusions from each essay. How are these two conclusions different from each other?

   ○ A. "Overcoming Impostor Syndrome" uses the conclusion to summarize ideas, while "Community Colleges vs. Technical Schools" uses it to ask readers reflective questions.
   ○ B. "Overcoming Impostor Syndrome" uses the conclusion to ask readers reflective questions, while "Community Colleges vs. Technical Schools" uses it to summarize ideas.
   ○ C. "Overcoming Impostor Syndrome" uses the conclusion to suggest further reading, while "Community Colleges vs. Technical Schools" uses it to summarize ideas.
   ○ D. "Overcoming Impostor Syndrome" uses the conclusion to ask the reader reflective questions, while "Community Colleges vs. Technical Schools" uses it to suggest further reading.

3. What do your answers to questions 1 and 2 tell you about the authors' approaches to their topics?

   ○ A. "Overcoming Impostor Syndrome" is more about taking action to help yourself, while "Community Colleges vs. Technical Schools" is more about processing information to make a decision.
   ○ B. "Overcoming Impostor Syndrome" is more about processing information to make a decision, while "Community Colleges vs. Technical Schools" is more about taking action to help yourself.
   ○ C. "Overcoming Impostor Syndrome" is more about taking action to help yourself, while "Community Colleges vs. Technical Schools" is more about helping others help themselves.
   ○ D. "Overcoming Impostor Syndrome" is more about doing research to master a subject, while "Community Colleges vs. Technical Schools" is more about processing information to make a decision.

Copyright © BookheadEd Learning, LLC

Please note that excerpts and passages in the StudySync® library and this workbook are intended as touchstones to generate interest in an author's work. The excerpts and passages do not substitute for the reading of entire texts, and StudySync® strongly recommends that students seek out and purchase the whole literary or informational work in order to experience it as the author intended. Links to online resellers are available in our digital library. In addition, complete works may be ordered through an authorized reseller by filling out and returning to StudySync® the order form enclosed in this workbook.

OVERCOMING
IMPOSTOR SYNDROME

Close Read

Reread "Overcoming Impostor Syndrome." As you reread, complete the Skills Focus questions below. Then use your answers and annotations from the questions to help you complete the Write activity.

◎ SKILLS FOCUS

1. Highlight an example of a specific kind of text structure that appears at least twice in "Overcoming Impostor Syndrome," and explain how using this type of structure helps make the author's points clear, convincing, and engaging.

2. Highlight a detail that supports a central idea in "Overcoming Impostor Syndrome," and explain why it is effective supporting evidence.

3. Highlight a paragraph that helped you identify text structure in "Overcoming Impostor Syndrome." Write a sentence that explains the relationship between the text structure and the main idea of the article.

4. Compare and contrast the use of sub-headings in both "Overcoming Impostor Syndrome" and "Community Colleges vs. Technical Schools". Using textual evidence from "Overcoming Impostor Syndrome" and your memory of "Community Colleges vs. Technical Schools", explain why the authors chose to use subheadings.

5. Both "Overcoming Impostor Syndrome" and "Community Colleges vs. Technical Schools" address decisions and mindsets that are important as high school seniors prepare for their future. How can the main ideas in these articles help you transform your own future?

✏ WRITE

RESEARCH: Select a topic related to your life after high school that you would like to learn more about (for example, how to find a job or how to select a dorm roommate). Then write an informational article about this topic, applying informational text structures to your article and to support your main idea or claim.

Copyright © BookheadEd Learning, LLC

Please note that excerpts and passages in the StudySync® library and this workbook are intended as touchstones to generate interest in an author's work. The excerpts and passages do not substitute for the reading of entire texts, and StudySync® strongly recommends that students seek out and purchase the whole literary or informational work in order to experience it as the author intended. Links to online resellers are available in our digital library. In addition, complete works may be ordered through an authorized reseller by filling out and returning to StudySync® the order form enclosed in this workbook.

Reading & Writing Companion   33

The
Metamorphosis

FICTION
Franz Kafka
1915

Introduction

studysync ⓥ

Czech author Franz Kafka (1883–1924) asked friend and biographer Max Brod to destroy his writings after he died, but Brod thought better of it—otherwise readers would be robbed of the brilliance of Kafka's dark vision. *The Metamorphosis* is typical of Kafka's work, with nightmarish themes of surrealism, confusion, and oppression. In this excerpt, Gregor Samsa awakens to find himself

'O God,' he thought, 'what a demanding job I've chosen!'

Copyright © BookheadEd Learning, LLC

1   One morning, as Gregor Samsa was waking up from anxious dreams, he discovered that in bed he had been changed into a monstrous verminous bug. He lay on his armour-hard back and saw, as he lifted his head up a little, his brown, arched abdomen divided up into rigid bow-like sections. From this height the blanket, just about ready to slide off completely, could hardly stay in place. His numerous legs, pitifully thin in comparison to the rest of his circumference, flickered helplessly before his eyes.

Franz Kafka, 1906

2   'What's happened to me,' he thought. It was no dream. His room, a proper room for a human being, only somewhat too small, lay quietly between the four well-known walls. Above the table, on which an unpacked collection of sample cloth goods was spread out (Samsa was a traveling salesman) hung the picture which he had cut out of an illustrated magazine a little while ago and set in a pretty gilt frame. It was a picture of a woman with a fur hat and a fur boa. She sat erect there, lifting up in the direction of the viewer a solid fur muff into which her entire forearm disappeared.

3   Gregor's glance then turned to the window. The dreary weather (the rain drops were falling audibly down on the metal window ledge) made him quite melancholy. 'Why don't I keep sleeping for a little while longer and forget all this foolishness,' he thought. But this was entirely impractical, for he was used to sleeping on his right side, and in his present state he couldn't get himself into this position. No matter how hard he threw himself onto his right side, he always rolled again onto his back. He must have tried it a hundred times, closing his eyes, so that he would not have to see the wriggling legs, and gave up only when he began to feel a light, dull pain in his side which he had never felt before.

NOTES

Skill:
Story Structure

Kafka begins the story after the metamorphosis has taken place. So I can assume that the story will be about living life as an insect rather than becoming one. This kind of beginning makes the story surprising and humorous.

Skill:
Connotation and Denotation

The words *proper* and *well-known* often have positive or neutral connotations, but I think Kafka might be implying a more negative connotation. I think the message might be that Gregor has had a rather mundane and monotonous life.

Please note that excerpts and passages in the StudySync® library and this workbook are intended as touchstones to generate interest in an author's work. The excerpts and passages do not substitute for the reading of entire texts, and StudySync® strongly recommends that students seek out and purchase the whole literary or informational work in order to experience it as the author intended. Links to online resellers are available in our digital library. In addition, complete works may be ordered through an authorized reseller by filling out and returning to StudySync® the order form enclosed in this workbook.

4 'O God,' he thought, 'what a demanding job I've chosen! Day in, day out on the road. The stresses of trade are much greater than the work going on at head office, and, in addition to that, I have to deal with the problems of traveling, the worries about train connections, irregular bad food, temporary and constantly changing human relationships which never come from the heart. To hell with it all!' He felt a slight itching on the top of his abdomen. He slowly pushed himself on his back closer to the bed post so that he could lift his head more easily, found the itchy part, which was entirely covered with small white spots (he did not know what to make of them), and wanted to feel the place with a leg. But he retracted it immediately, for the contact felt like a cold shower all over him.

5 He slid back again into his earlier position. 'This getting up early,' he thought, 'makes a man quite idiotic. A man must have his sleep. Other traveling salesmen live like harem women. For **instance**, when I come back to the inn during the course of the morning to write up the necessary orders, these gentlemen are just sitting down to breakfast. If I were to try that with my boss, I'd be thrown out on the spot. Still, who knows whether that mightn't be really good for me. If I didn't hold back for my parents' sake, I would've quit ages ago. I would've gone to the boss and told him just what I think from the bottom of my heart. He would've fallen right off his desk! How weird it is to sit up at the desk and talk down to the employee from way up there. The boss has trouble hearing, so the employee has to step up quite close to him. Anyway, I haven't completely given up that hope yet. Once I've got together the money to pay off the parents' debt to him—that should take another five or six years—I'll do it for su[re. Then I'll make the big break. In any case, right now I have to get up. My train leaves at five o'clock.'

6 And he looked over at the alarm clock ticking away by the chest of drawers. 'Good God,' he thought. It was half past six, and the hands were going quietly on. It was past the half hour, already nearly quarter to. Could the alarm have failed to ring? One saw from the bed that it was properly set for four o'clock. Certainly it had rung. Yes, but was it possible to sleep through this noise that made the furniture shake? Now, it's true he'd not slept quietly, but evidently he'd slept all the more deeply. Still, what should he do now? The next train left at seven o'clock. To catch that one, he would have to go in a mad rush. The sample collection wasn't packed up yet, and he really didn't feel particularly fresh and active. And even if he caught the train, there was no avoiding a blow up with the boss, because the firm's errand boy would've waited for the five o'clock train and reported the news of his absence long ago. He was the boss's minion, without backbone or intelligence. Well then, what if he reported in sick? But that would be extremely embarrassing and **suspicious**, because during his five years' service Gregor hadn't been sick even once. The boss

Copyright © BookheadEd Learning, LLC

Please note that excerpts and passages in the StudySync® library and this workbook are intended as touchstones to generate interest in an author's work. The excerpts and passages do not substitute for the reading of entire texts, and StudySync® strongly recommends that students seek out and purchase the whole literary or informational work in order to experience it as the author intended. Links to online resellers are available in our digital library. In addition, complete works may be ordered through an authorized reseller by filling out and returning to StudySync® the order form enclosed in this workbook.

would certainly come with the doctor from the health insurance company and would reproach his parents for their lazy son and cut short all objections with the insurance doctor's comments; for him everyone was completely healthy but really lazy about work. And besides, would the doctor in this case be totally wrong? Apart from a really excessive drowsiness after the long sleep, Gregor in fact felt quite well and even had a really strong appetite.

7   As he was thinking all this over in the greatest haste, without being able to make the decision to get out of bed (the alarm clock was indicating exactly quarter to seven) there was a cautious knock on the door by the head of the bed.

8   'Gregor,' a voice called (it was his mother!) 'it's quarter to seven. Don't you want to be on your way?' The soft voice! Gregor was startled when he heard his voice answering. It was clearly and unmistakably his earlier voice, but in it was intermingled, as if from below, an irrepressibly painful squeaking which left the words positively distinct only in the first moment and distorted them in the reverberation, so that one didn't know if one had heard correctly. Gregor wanted to answer in detail and explain everything, but in these circumstances he **confined** himself to saying, 'Yes, yes, thank you mother. I'm getting up right away.' Because of the wooden door the change in Gregor's voice was not really noticeable outside, so his mother calmed down with this explanation and shuffled off. However, as a result of the short conversation the other family members became aware of the fact that Gregor was unexpectedly still at home, and already his father was knocking on one side door, weakly but with his fist. 'Gregor, Gregor,' he called out, 'what's going on?' And after a short while he urged him on again in a deeper voice. 'Gregor!' Gregor!' At the other side door, however, his sister knocked lightly. 'Gregor? Are you all right? Do you need anything?' Gregor directed answers in both directions, 'I'll be ready right away.' He made an effort with the most careful articulation and by inserting long pauses between the individual words to remove everything remarkable from his voice. His father turned back to his breakfast. However, the sister whispered, 'Gregor, open the door, I beg you.' Gregor had no intention of opening the door, but congratulated himself on his precaution, acquired from traveling, of locking all doors during the night, even at home.

9   First he wanted to stand up quietly and undisturbed, get dressed, above all have breakfast, and only then consider further action, for (he noticed this clearly) by thinking things over in bed he would not reach a reasonable conclusion. He remembered that he had already often felt a light pain or other in bed, perhaps the result of an awkward lying position, which later turned out to be purely imaginary when he stood up, and he was eager to see how his present fantasies would gradually dissipate. That the change in his voice was nothing other than the onset of a real chill, an occupational illness of commercial travelers, of that he had not the slightest doubt.

Skill:
Textual Evidence

The exclamation mark might indicate that Gregor is surprised by his mother's voice. But why? Maybe he hears differently now that he is a bug. Or perhaps it gives him comfort in his current condition. I'll need to read more.

Copyright © BookheadEd Learning, LLC

Please note that excerpts and passages in the StudySync® library and this workbook are intended as touchstones to generate interest in an author's work. The excerpts and passages do not substitute for the reading of entire texts, and StudySync® strongly recommends that students seek out and purchase the whole literary or informational work in order to experience it as the author intended. Links to online resellers are available in our digital library. In addition, complete works may be ordered through an authorized reseller by filling out and returning to StudySync® the order form enclosed in this workbook.

10   It was very easy to throw aside the blanket. He needed only to push himself up a little, and it fell by itself. But to continue was difficult, particularly because he was so unusually wide. He needed arms and hands to push himself upright. Instead of these, however, he had only many small limbs which were **incessantly** moving with very different motions and which, in addition, he was unable to control. If he wanted to bend one of them, then it was the first to extend itself, and if he finally succeeded doing with this limb what he wanted, in the meantime all the others, as if left free, moved around in an excessively painful agitation. 'But I must not stay in bed uselessly,' said Gregor to himself.

11   At first he wanted to get of the bed with the lower part of his body, but this lower part (which he incidentally had not yet looked at and which he also couldn't picture clearly) proved itself too difficult to move. The attempt went so slowly. When, having become almost frantic, he finally hurled himself forward with all his force and without thinking, he chose his direction incorrectly, and he hit the lower bedpost hard. The violent pain he felt revealed to him that the lower part of his body was at the moment probably the most sensitive.

12   Thus, he tried to get his upper body out of the bed first and turned his head carefully toward the edge of the bed. He managed to do this easily, and in spite of its width and weight his body mass at last slowly followed the turning of his head. But as he finally raised his head outside the bed in the open air, he became anxious about moving forward any further in this manner, for if he allowed himself eventually to fall by this process, it would take a miracle to prevent his head from getting injured. And at all costs he must not lose consciousness right now. He preferred to remain in bed.

13   However, after a similar effort, while he lay there again sighing as before and once again saw his small limbs fighting one another, if anything worse than before, and didn't see any chance of imposing quiet and order on this **arbitrary** movement, he told himself again that he couldn't possibly remain in bed and that it might be the most reasonable thing to sacrifice everything if there was even the slightest hope of getting himself out of bed in the process. At the same moment, however, he didn't forget to remind himself from time to time of the fact that calm (indeed the calmest) reflection might be better than the most confused decisions. At such moments, he directed his gaze as precisely as he could toward the window, but unfortunately there was little confident cheer to be had from a glance at the morning mist, which concealed even the other side of the narrow street. 'It's already seven o'clock' he told himself at the latest striking of the alarm clock, 'already seven o'clock and still such a fog.' And for a little while longer he lay quietly with weak breathing, as if perhaps waiting for normal and natural conditions to re-emerge out of the complete stillness.

Copyright © BookheadEd Learning, LLC

Please note that excerpts and passages in the StudySync® library and this workbook are intended as touchstones to generate interest in an author's work. The excerpts and passages do not substitute for the reading of entire texts, and StudySync® strongly recommends that students seek out and purchase the whole literary or informational work in order to experience it as the author intended. Links to online resellers are available in our digital library. In addition, complete works may be ordered through an authorized reseller by filling out and returning to StudySync® the order form enclosed in this workbook.

First Read

Read *The Metamorphosis*. After you read, complete the Think Questions below.

☁ THINK QUESTIONS

1. Is Gregor's transformation real or imagined? How does Kafka's writing style affect the believability of the story? Explain your reasoning in a few sentences, including specific examples from the text.

2. What is Gregor Samsa's attitude toward his chosen work as a traveling salesman? Use evidence from the text to explain his feelings about his job and his place in society.

3. Is Gregor's "metamorphosis" an inexplicable occurrence? Or does Kafka give any clues or insights to suggest why this may have happened or what might have caused it? Cite specific examples from the excerpt in your response.

4. Use context clues to determine the meaning of **confined** as it is used in paragraph 8 of *The Metamorphosis*. Write your definition of *confined* here and explain which context clues helped you determine its meaning.

5. The Latin verb cessare means "to cease or stop." Knowing this, along with any other common affixes and/or roots, what do you think the adverb **incessantly** means? Write your best definition here, along with any other related words with a similar origin.

Copyright © BookheadEd Learning, LLC

Please note that excerpts and passages in the StudySync® library and this workbook are intended as touchstones to generate interest in an author's work. The excerpts and passages do not substitute for the reading of entire texts, and StudySync® strongly recommends that students seek out and purchase the whole literary or informational work in order to experience it as the author intended. Links to online resellers are available in our digital library. In addition, complete works may be ordered through an authorized reseller by filling out and returning to StudySync® the order form enclosed in this workbook.

Reading & Writing Companion   **39**

Skill:
Story Structure

Use the Checklist to analyze Story Structure in *The Metamorphosis*. Refer to the sample student annotations about Story Structure in the text.

••• CHECKLIST FOR STORY STRUCTURE

In order to identify the choices an author makes when structuring specific parts of a text, note the following:

✓ the choices an author makes to organize specific parts of a text such as where to begin and end a story, or whether the ending should be tragic, comic, or inconclusive

✓ the author's use of literary devices, such as:

- foreshadowing: a way of hinting at what will come later
- flashback: a part of a story that shows something that happened in the past
- pacing: how quickly or slowly the events of a story unfold

✓ how the overall structure of the text contributes to its meaning as well as its aesthetic impact

- the effect structure has on the impact it makes on the reader, such as the creation of suspense through the use of pacing
- the use of flashback to reveal hidden dimensions of a character that affect the theme

To analyze how an author's choices concerning how to structure specific parts of a text contribute to its overall structure and meaning as well as its aesthetic impact, consider the following questions:

✓ How does the author structure the text overall? How does the author structure specific parts of the text?

✓ Does the author incorporate literary elements such as flashback or foreshadowing?

✓ How do these elements affect the overall text structure and the aesthetic impact of the text?

Copyright © BookheadEd Learning, LLC

Please note that excerpts and passages in the StudySync® library and this workbook are intended as touchstones to generate interest in an author's work. The excerpts and passages do not substitute for the reading of entire texts, and StudySync® strongly recommends that students seek out and purchase the whole literary or informational work in order to experience it as the author intended. Links to online resellers are available in our digital library. In addition, complete works may be ordered through an authorized reseller by filling out and returning to StudySync® the order form enclosed in this workbook.

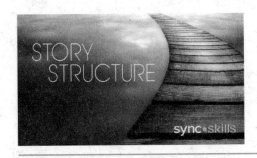

Skill: Story Structure

Reread paragraph 5 of *The Metamorphosis*. Then, using the Checklist on the previous page, answer the multiple-choice questions below.

↻ YOUR TURN

1. Which of the following sentences is most likely to be an example of foreshadowing?

   ○ A. "This getting up early," he thought, "makes a man quite idiotic."
   ○ B. Other traveling salesmen live like harem women.
   ○ C. For **instance**, when I come back to the inn during the course of the morning to write up the necessary orders, these gentlemen are just sitting down to breakfast.
   ○ D. If I were to try that with my boss, I'd be thrown out on the spot.

2. What is the most likely reason that Kafka has his main character mention his parents' debt before the parents appear in the story?

   ○ A. So the reader will understand why Gregor was turned into a bug-like creature.
   ○ B. So the reader will learn about the relationship between Gregor and his parents.
   ○ C. So the reader will understand how poor Gregor's family is and feel bad for them.
   ○ D. So the reader will learn about the social structures that were prevalent at the time in which this story is set.

3. This passage consists largely of a long, unhurried series of thoughts from Gregor Samsa. What is the most likely reason Kafka uses such slow pacing at the opening of this story?

   ○ A. It helps the reader understand precisely how Gregor feels about the other traveling salesmen he regularly encounters.
   ○ B. It helps reveal many aspects of Gregor's life, and it helps reveal the absurdity of his fear of losing his job when he should be more concerned about being a bug.
   ○ C. It helps the reader understand that this story might become monotonous, with long, drawn-out passages consisting largely of Gregor's thoughts.
   ○ D. It helps reveal the author's feelings about common vices, such as laziness and uncleanliness.

Copyright © BookheadEd Learning, LLC

Please note that excerpts and passages in the StudySync® library and this workbook are intended as touchstones to generate interest in an author's work. The excerpts and passages do not substitute for the reading of entire texts, and StudySync® strongly recommends that students seek out and purchase the whole literary or informational work in order to experience it as the author intended. Links to online resellers are available in our digital library. In addition, complete works may be ordered through an authorized reseller by filling out and returning to StudySync® the order form enclosed in this workbook.

Skill:
Textual Evidence

Use the Checklist to analyze Textual Evidence in *The Metamorphosis*. Refer to the sample student annotations about Textual Evidence in the text.

••• CHECKLIST FOR STORY STRUCTURE

In order to support an analysis by citing evidence that is explicitly stated in the text, do the following:

- ✓ read the text closely and critically
- ✓ identify what the text says explicitly
- ✓ find the most relevant textual evidence that supports your analysis
- ✓ consider why an author explicitly states specific details and information
- ✓ cite the specific words, phrases, sentences, or paragraphs from the text that support your analysis
- ✓ determine where evidence in the text still leaves certain matters uncertain or unresolved

In order to interpret implicit meanings in a text by making inferences, do the following:

- ✓ combine information directly stated in the text with your own knowledge, experiences, and observations
- ✓ cite the specific words, phrases, sentences, or paragraphs from the text that led to and support this inference.

In order to cite textual evidence to support an analysis of what the text says explicitly as well as inferences drawn from the text, consider the following questions:

- ✓ Have I read the text closely and critically?
- ✓ What inferences am I making about the text?
- ✓ What textual evidence am I using to support these inferences?
- ✓ Am I quoting the evidence from the text correctly?
- ✓ Does my textual evidence logically relate to my analysis or the inference I am making?
- ✓ Does evidence in the text still leave certain matters unanswered or unresolved? In what ways?

Copyright © BookheadEd Learning, LLC

Please note that excerpts and passages in the StudySync® library and this workbook are intended as touchstones to generate interest in an author's work. The excerpts and passages do not substitute for the reading of entire texts, and StudySync® strongly recommends that students seek out and purchase the whole literary or informational work in order to experience it as the author intended. Links to online resellers are available in our digital library. In addition, complete works may be ordered through an authorized reseller by filling out and returning to StudySync® the order form enclosed in this workbook.

Skill:
Textual Evidence

Reread paragraph 9 of *The Metamorphosis*. Then, using the Checklist on the previous page, answer the multiple-choice questions below.

⟳ YOUR TURN

1. Which of the following sentences would provide the best textual evidence for the inference that Gregor Samsa still doesn't want to believe he has turned into a bug?

   ○ A. "First he wanted to stand up quietly and undisturbed, get dressed, above all have breakfast, and only then consider further action . . ."

   ○ B. ". . . for (he noticed this clearly) by thinking things over in bed he would not reach a reasonable conclusion."

   ○ C. "He remembered that he had already often felt a light pain or other in bed . . ."

   ○ D. "That the change in his voice was nothing other than the onset of a real chill, an occupational illness of commercial travelers, of that he had not the slightest doubt."

Copyright © BookheadEd Learning, LLC

Please note that excerpts and passages in the StudySync® library and this workbook are intended as touchstones to generate interest in an author's work. The excerpts and passages do not substitute for the reading of entire texts, and StudySync® strongly recommends that students seek out and purchase the whole literary or informational work in order to experience it as the author intended. Links to online resellers are available in our digital library. In addition, complete works may be ordered through an authorized reseller by filling out and returning to StudySync® the order form enclosed in this workbook.

Reading & Writing
Companion

43

Read the inferences in the chart below. Then, complete the chart by matching the textual evidence that best supports each inference.

↻ YOUR TURN

	Textual Evidence Options
A	He remembered that he had already often felt a light pain or other in bed, perhaps the result of an awkward lying position . . .
B	. . . above all have breakfast, and only then consider further action . . .
C	. . . he was eager to see how his present fantasies would gradually dissipate.
D	First he wanted to stand up quietly and undisturbed . . .

Inference	Textual Evidence
Gregor doesn't reason well on an empty stomach.	
Gregor has previously had trouble sleeping.	
Gregor wants to keep his condition secret.	
Gregor does not believe he is actually a bug.	

Copyright © BookheadEd Learning, LLC

Please note that excerpts and passages in the StudySync® library and this workbook are intended as touchstones to generate interest in an author's work. The excerpts and passages do not substitute for the reading of entire texts, and StudySync® strongly recommends that students seek out and purchase the whole literary or informational work in order to experience it as the author intended. Links to online resellers are available in our digital library. In addition, complete works may be ordered through an authorized reseller by filling out and returning to StudySync® the order form enclosed in this workbook.

Skill: Connotation and Denotation

Use the Checklist to analyze Connotation and Denotation in *The Metamorphosis*. Refer to the sample student annotations about Connotation and Denotation in the text.

••• CHECKLIST FOR CONNOTATION AND DENOTATION

In order to identify the denotative meanings of words, use the following steps:

- ✓ first, note unfamiliar words and phrases, key words used to describe important characters, events, and ideas, or words that inspire an emotional reaction

- ✓ next, determine and note the denotative meaning of words by consulting a reference material such as a dictionary, glossary, or thesaurus

- ✓ finally, analyze nuances in the meaning of words with similar denotations

To better understand the meaning of words and phrases as they are used in a text, including connotative meanings, use the following questions as a guide

- ✓ What is the genre or subject of the text? Based on context, what do you think the meaning of the word is intended to be?

- ✓ Is your inference the same or different from the dictionary definition?

- ✓ Does the word create a positive, negative, or neutral emotion?

- ✓ What synonyms or alternative phrasing help you describe the connotative meaning of the word?

To determine the meaning of words and phrases as they are used in a text, including connotative meanings, use the following questions as a guide:

- ✓ What is the denotative meaning of the word? Is that denotative meaning correct in context?

- ✓ What possible positive, neutral, or negative connotations might the word have, depending on context?

- ✓ What textual evidence signals a particular connotation for the word?

Copyright © BookheadEd Learning, LLC

Please note that excerpts and passages in the StudySync® library and this workbook are intended as touchstones to generate interest in an author's work. The excerpts and passages do not substitute for the reading of entire texts, and StudySync® strongly recommends that students seek out and purchase the whole literary or informational work in order to experience it as the author intended. Links to online resellers are available in our digital library. In addition, complete works may be ordered through an authorized reseller by filling out and returning to StudySync® the order form enclosed in this workbook.

Skill: Connotation and Denotation

Reread paragraph 13 of *The Metamorphosis*. Then, using the Checklist on the previous page, answer the multiple-choice questions below.

↻ YOUR TURN

1. Which of the following words is most likely to have a negative connotation in the context of this passage?

   ○ A. confidence
   ○ B. cheer
   ○ C. concealed
   ○ D. street

2. Which word in the passage can be interpreted figuratively, and with a negative connotation, to describe unclear thinking?

   ○ A. gaze
   ○ B. window
   ○ C. street
   ○ D. fog

3. Which of the following denotative meanings of *fog* best fits how the word is used in this paragraph?

   ○ A. a thick cloud close to the earth's surface
   ○ B. to cover with steam
   ○ C. to treat something with a spray
   ○ D. something that confuses a thought process

Please note that excerpts and passages in the StudySync® library and this workbook are intended as touchstones to generate interest in an author's work. The excerpts and passages do not substitute for the reading of entire texts, and StudySync® strongly recommends that students seek out and purchase the whole literary or informational work in order to experience it as the author intended. Links to online resellers are available in our digital library. In addition, complete works may be ordered through an authorized reseller by filling out and returning to StudySync® the order form enclosed in this workbook.

Copyright © BookheadEd Learning, LLC

Close Read

Reread *The Metamorphosis*. As you reread, complete the Skills Focus questions below. Then use your answers and annotations from the questions to help you complete the Write activity.

◎ SKILLS FOCUS

1. This excerpt, which is the very beginning of Kafka's *The Metamorphosis*, focuses on the main character's first morning as a "monstrous verminous bug." Why do you think Kafka chooses to spend so much time on this particular moment of the character's day? What effect does this have on the reader? Highlight and annotate details in the text that show how Kafka uses this moment in the character's day to develop the plot.

2. Throughout the passage, Gregor Samsa expresses his feelings about his job. Highlight three pieces of textual evidence that implicitly or explicitly inform you about Samsa's feelings toward his work, his colleagues, and his boss. Annotate your highlights to explain what this textual evidence helps you understand about Samsa and his job.

3. Find and highlight three words in this excerpt that tell you (through connotation or denotation) how Samsa feels about his family members. Use the annotation feature to explain what these words tell you about this feelings toward his family members.

4. Gregor Samsa wakes up to an incredible transformation. Highlight and annotate textual evidence to support your response to the following questions: What aspects of Samsa's life was he unable to change before this moment? In what ways was Samsa unable to transform his own future? How will his transformation into a "monstrous verminous bug" change his future?

✏ WRITE

LITERARY ANALYSIS: An allegory is a literary device used to convey a symbolic message that comments on some aspect of human life and society. In an allegory, characters represent ideas. Kafka uses the literary device of allegory to structure this story. What do you think the character of Gregor Samsa represents? What message might the author be conveying about human life and society? Focus on specific words that connote or denote an opinion about human life and society. Use textual evidence to support your ideas.

Copyright © BookheadEd Learning, LLC

Please note that excerpts and passages in the StudySync® library and this workbook are intended as touchstones to generate interest in an author's work. The excerpts and passages do not substitute for the reading of entire texts, and StudySync® strongly recommends that students seek out and purchase the whole literary or informational work in order to experience it as the author intended. Links to online resellers are available in our digital library. In addition, complete works may be ordered through an authorized reseller by filling out and returning to StudySync® the order form enclosed in this workbook.

Reading & Writing Companion   47

Blast: In Your Hands

What are the challenges of planning for life after high school?

(i) BACKGROUND

Listen to the What's Next podcast associated with this Blast in your digital account.

Are you a high school student? If so, you've probably fantasized about what it will be like to walk across the stage in a tasseled cap and long gown, proudly accepting a diploma after 13 years of hard work. But how much have you thought about what will happen after you step off the stage?

Finishing high school is a momentous achievement that many anticipate eagerly, but it can be tougher to picture what life will look like after graduation.

Every year, more than 3 million American students graduate high school, according to the National Center for Education Statistics. Nationwide, seniors are faced with questions they have never confronted face-to-face before: What will I do once I finish high school? How will I chase my passions, and what am I passionate about? What does my future hold? It can feel scary and intimidating when all these questions lie ahead. Luckily, there are countless resources to help you along the way. Some of the most valuable resources are people who have gone through the process themselves.

StudySync's "What's Next?" Blast and podcast series follows ten high school students — nine seniors, one junior — from September to May. Throughout the year, StudySync documents these students as they encountered the challenges of planning for life after high school. From an aspiring esthetician eager to start her career in California to a risk-taking Texan with his sights set

Copyright © BookheadEd Learning, LLC

Please note that excerpts and passages in the StudySync® library and this workbook are intended as touchstones to generate interest in an author's work. The excerpts and passages do not substitute for the reading of entire texts, and StudySync® strongly recommends that students seek out and purchase the whole literary or informational work in order to experience it as the author intended. Links to online resellers are available in our digital library. In addition, complete works may be ordered through an authorized reseller by filling out and returning to StudySync® the order form enclosed in this workbook.

on a private university, these seven students have a wide variety of backgrounds, interests, motivations, and goals. Their advice can help you start answering some of the toughest questions you face as you decide your next steps. Listening to their stories can help you start planning your own.

Below, read a brief description and listen to a one-minute audio clip introducing each student.

Diana-Nicole Ramirez is a senior at the Academy of Finance and Enterprise in Queens, New York. She loves reading, writing, and classic rock. After graduating, she plans to attend college in New York City to study journalism and communications.

DJ Frost is a senior at Blue Springs South High School in Blue Springs, Missouri. After graduation, he plans to attend the Air Force Academy in Colorado to play football and major in business.

Felicia Horn is a senior at Paul VI High School in Haddonfield, New Jersey. Inspired by hospital visits with her mom, who has multiple sclerosis, Horn aspires to be a nurse, and eventually a nurse anesthetist.

Katherine Carlo is a senior at Nease High School in St. Augustine, Florida. She's applying to schools in Florida and the surrounding states, as well as Ivy League schools, and hopes to get a scholarship to pay for college.

Kiana Griffin is a senior at Pleasant Grove High School in Elk Grove, California. After graduation, she hopes to play basketball at a D1 university.

Lyssa Nix is a senior at Classical Academy High School in Escondido, California. After graduation, she will attend cosmetology school to become an esthetician and begin a career close to home.

Makalya Adams is a senior at William B. Murrah High School in Jackson, Mississippi. She aspires to become a nurse, and is torn between attending a local community college, which she prefers, or a local private college, which her mom thinks is best.

Patrick Cadogan is a junior at Westford Academy in Westford, Massachusetts. With the goal of attending a four-year college in-state, he will spend this year taking the SAT, building a strong application and narrowing down where he would like to apply.

Shamora Rogers is a senior at Warren High School in San Antonio, Texas. She is applying to four-year public universities in state and is excited to study theater, film, and television in college.

Copyright © BookheadEd Learning, LLC

Please note that excerpts and passages in the StudySync® library and this workbook are intended as touchstones to generate interest in an author's work. The excerpts and passages do not substitute for the reading of entire texts, and StudySync® strongly recommends that students seek out and purchase the whole literary or informational work in order to experience it as the author intended. Links to online resellers are available in our digital library. In addition, complete works may be ordered through an authorized reseller by filling out and returning to StudySync® the order form enclosed in this workbook.

NOTES

Zac Walsdorf is a senior at John Marshall High School in San Antonio, Texas. A student with many interests and a love for trying new things, he plans to apply to various elite private universities out of state.

After listening to each of the students at the start of their school year, whom do you relate to most? Did any of their comments resonate with you? What are the biggest obstacles that lie ahead in your journey toward adult life? What are the challenges of planning for life after high school?

NUMBER CRUNCH

45

◔ QUIKPOLL

Do you feel prepared for adult life?

☐ Absolutely. I've been waiting for high school graduation for years, and I couldn't be more ready. I can't wait for the next steps.

☐ Mostly. I know I have the skills I need for adult life, but I'm also a little nervous.

☐ Not really. I'm excited for the future, but I know I still have a lot of preparing to do.

☐ Not at all. I'm terrified for adult life. Do I have to graduate?

✹ CREATE YOUR BLAST

What are the challenges of planning for life after high school?

_____

_____

_____

_____

Copyright © BookheadEd Learning, LLC

Please note that excerpts and passages in the StudySync® library and this workbook are intended as touchstones to generate interest in an author's work. The excerpts and passages do not substitute for the reading of entire texts, and StudySync® strongly recommends that students seek out and purchase the whole literary or informational work in order to experience it as the author intended. Links to online resellers are available in our digital library. In addition, complete works may be ordered through an authorized reseller by filling out and returning to StudySync® the order form enclosed in this workbook.

Blast: The Future Awaits

What do you want to do after you graduate high school?

BACKGROUND

Listen to the What's Next podcast associated with this Blast in your digital account.

When you imagine your life five years from now, what do you picture?

Do you envision yourself as a newly minted college graduate launching a career in your dream industry, or a passionate volunteer traveling the world and serving those less fortunate? Maybe you see yourself rising in rank in the military, building a business, saving money for the future, or starting a family. Perhaps you're totally uncertain about what your life will look like — after all, how can you know what you'll be doing years down the road when you're still trying to navigate the immediate day-to-day challenges of high school?

Selecting a course of action after graduation — whether it's college, employment, volunteering, a gap year, or something else — is one of the most consequential decisions most seniors in high school have ever made, so it's normal to be overwhelmed and unsure, according to Kristen Flemer, a counselor at Skyline High School in Sammamish, Washington.

Flemer says one way to start narrowing down future plans is to reflect on what you enjoy doing now. "Start with questions," she said. "What do you love? What do you do on the weekends? If you could do one thing for the rest of your life, what would you do? What do you not like doing? Would you rather be outdoors or indoors? Would you rather be on a computer or talking with someone? Would you rather be up and moving or sitting at a desk?" Once

Copyright © BookheadEd Learning, LLC

Please note that excerpts and passages in the StudySync® library and this workbook are intended as touchstones to generate interest in an author's work. The excerpts and passages do not substitute for the reading of entire texts, and StudySync® strongly recommends that students seek out and purchase the whole literary or informational work in order to experience it as the author intended. Links to online resellers are available in our digital library. In addition, complete works may be ordered through an authorized reseller by filling out and returning to StudySync® the order form enclosed in this workbook.

Reading & Writing Companion   51

NOTES

you've identified and solidified goals for a future lifestyle, Flemer says, you can figure out a career that suits those goals, and work backwards to devise an action plan for how to arrive at that lifestyle.

It might seem like all your peers are pursuing the same path after high school, but that doesn't necessarily have to mean this path is right for you — and Kelly Kaye, the operations manager of a financial planning firm in Los Angeles, knows this firsthand. When she was a senior in high school in Buffalo, New York, most of her friends were pursuing college degrees at expensive and elite private universities. However, her family didn't have the financial means to afford that kind of education, so Kaye created a new plan: She moved to California after graduating high school, worked at a bank to save money and establish residency in the state, and then enrolled a year later in community college in Santa Monica. From there, she transferred to a state university and earned a Bachelor's degree. Even though Kaye opted for a different path than her friends, she gained independence, made money over the course of a gap year, and ended up in a career she enjoys. "Listen to what other people have to say, but don't make your decision based on somebody else's opinion," Kaye says. "Do what feels right to you, even if that's going against the grain."

So, do you see yourself going to college, pursuing a career, joining the military, working to save for college, or something else? Have you already crafted a plan for life after graduation, or are you still weighing options? What do you want to do after you graduate high school?

NUMBER CRUNCH

69.7

⦿ QUIKPOLL

Which of the following best fits your plan for life after graduation?

☐ Four-year college

☐ Two-year college or trade school

☐ Gap year, traveling, or joining the military

☐ Working

☐ Something else

Please note that excerpts and passages in the StudySync® library and this workbook are intended as touchstones to generate interest in an author's work. The excerpts and passages do not substitute for the reading of entire texts, and StudySync® strongly recommends that students seek out and purchase the whole literary or informational work in order to experience it as the author intended. Links to online resellers are available in our digital library. In addition, complete works may be ordered through an authorized reseller by filling out and returning to StudySync® the order form enclosed in this workbook.

Copyright © BookheadEd Learning, LLC

✴ CREATE YOUR BLAST

What do you want to do after you graduate high school?

_____

_____

_____

_____

Copyright © BookheadEd Learning, LLC

Please note that excerpts and passages in the StudySync® library and this workbook are intended as touchstones to generate interest in an author's work. The excerpts and passages do not substitute for the reading of entire texts, and StudySync® strongly recommends that students seek out and purchase the whole literary or informational work in order to experience it as the author intended. Links to online resellers are available in our digital library. In addition, complete works may be ordered through an authorized reseller by filling out and returning to StudySync® the order form enclosed in this workbook.

Reading & Writing
Companion

53

Blast: Your Perfect Path

What are the benefits of college alternatives?

ⓘ BACKGROUND

Listen to the What's Next podcast associated with this Blast in your digital account.

In 1980 in Anchorage, Alaska, a young man named Mark Begich graduated from high school. While some of his peers chased dreams of higher education, Begich pursued a different path.

Already a thriving entrepreneur, Begich chose not to go to college. Instead, he began managing his family's real estate properties. He also grew his own businesses, including a jewelry business and an 18-and-under club in Anchorage that he had run since the age of 14. As he became more successful in business over the years, he grew more involved in local politics as well. Eventually, he became the city's mayor. In 2008, Begich took his political aspirations even further, campaigning for the United States Senate. When he won, Begich became the only sitting U.S. senator without a college degree.

During your senior year of high school, it might seem like you have to go to college in order to be successful in a career one day. However, the reality is that plenty of Americans, including former U.S. Senator Mark Begich, have flourished professionally without graduating from college. College is a popular path because it allows students to deepen their education, make connections, and obtain a certificate that some jobs require. Still, other options like career and technical education or employment can be just as beneficial — and at a much lower cost.

Copyright © BookheadEd Learning, LLC

Please note that excerpts and passages in the StudySync® library and this workbook are intended as touchstones to generate interest in an author's work. The excerpts and passages do not substitute for the reading of entire texts, and StudySync® strongly recommends that students seek out and purchase the whole literary or informational work in order to experience it as the author intended. Links to online resellers are available in our digital library. In addition, complete works may be ordered through an authorized reseller by filling out and returning to StudySync® the order form enclosed in this workbook.

NOTES

For students who don't have the financial means or academic record needed to attend college, or for students whose career goals don't require a higher degree, it can be wise to consider options besides college after high school. For example, career and technical education — sometimes called trade school or vocational school — can teach specific technical skills needed for a particular job. Career and technical education can usually be completed in a shorter period of time than traditional college and at a lower cost. These programs can certify people to pursue industrial careers, like becoming an electrician or a welder. They can also train people in the arts or in hands-on careers, like culinary arts or cosmetology.

If you're not sure whether you want to go to college yet, or want a break before jumping back into school, a gap year is another option. Tens of thousands of American students take advantage of a gap year every year. The American Gap Association defines a gap year as "a structured period of time when students take a break from formal education to increase self-awareness, learn from different cultures, and experiment with possible careers. Typically, these are achieved by a combination of traveling, volunteering, interning, or working." While gap years are particularly common in Europe and Australia, they have gained popularity in the U.S. in recent years. Ethan Knight, founder of the American Gap Association, says "everybody stands to benefit from a gap year." However, he advises students to think carefully and seek out resources to decide whether or not it's the right decision for them.

With the emphasis placed on college in America's high schools today, it can seem like everyone is applying to college. Begich encourages students to consider college as an option, but he also points out that success in life can be reached without a degree. "If you have the ability, with or without a college degree, you can achieve great things," he said. "If you decide not to go to college, don't let people make it sound like it's a bad thing. You have choices in life, you made a choice, and now you're going to take it to a new level."

So, what do you think? Have you ever thought that college might not be the right fit for you? Why might students consider a path besides college after high school? What are the benefits of college alternatives?

NUMBER CRUNCH
30,000 TO 40,000

Copyright © BookheadEd Learning, LLC

Please note that excerpts and passages in the StudySync® library and this workbook are intended as touchstones to generate interest in an author's work. The excerpts and passages do not substitute for the reading of entire texts, and StudySync® strongly recommends that students seek out and purchase the whole literary or informational work in order to experience it as the author intended. Links to online resellers are available in our digital library. In addition, complete works may be ordered through an authorized reseller by filling out and returning to StudySync® the order form enclosed in this workbook.

⏱ QUIKPOLL

Have you considered pursuing career and technical education in place of a two-year or four-year degree?

☐ Yes. I have thought about career and technical education as an alternative that might suit my current situation and career goals.

☐ No, but I might look into it. I am curious to see whether career and technical education could be a good fit for me.

☐ No. Based on what I want to do in the future, career and technical education is not the right path for me.

✳ CREATE YOUR BLAST

What are the benefits of college alternatives?

_____

_____

_____

_____

Copyright © BookheadEd Learning, LLC

Please note that excerpts and passages in the StudySync® library and this workbook are intended as touchstones to generate interest in an author's work. The excerpts and passages do not substitute for the reading of entire texts, and StudySync® strongly recommends that students seek out and purchase the whole literary or informational work in order to experience it as the author intended. Links to online resellers are available in our digital library. In addition, complete works may be ordered through an authorized reseller by filling out and returning to StudySync® the order form enclosed in this workbook.

Bird by Bird:
Some Instructions on Writing and Life

INFORMATIONAL TEXT
Anne Lamott
1995

Introduction

Anne Lamott (b. 1954) is a *New York Times* bestselling author who has written several books and novels. In addition to her fictional work, Lamott is known for her books aimed at imparting writing advice to aspiring writers. In this excerpt from *Bird by Bird: Some Instructions on Writing and Life*, Lamott describes what happens in her mind when she sits down to write, and how she deals with the sometimes overwhelming nature of her thoughts.

"Bird by bird, buddy. Just take it bird by bird."

NOTES

1   Often when you sit down to write, what you have in mind is an autobiographical novel about your childhood, or a play about the immigrant experience, or a history of—oh, say—say women. But this is like trying to **scale** a glacier. It's hard to get your footing, and your fingertips get all red and frozen and torn up. Then your mental illnesses arrive at the desk like your sickest, most secretive relatives. And they pull up chairs in a semicircle around the computer, and they try to be quiet but you know they are there with their weird coppery breath, leering at you behind your back.

2   What I do at this point, as the panic mounts and the jungle drums begin beating and I realize that the well has run dry and that my future is behind me and I'm going to have to get a job only I'm completely unemployable, is to stop. First I try to breathe, because I'm either sitting there panting like a lapdog or I'm unintentionally making slow asthmatic death rattles. So I just sit there for a minute, breathing slowly, quietly. I let my mind wander. After a moment I may notice that I'm trying to decide whether or not I am too old for orthodontia and whether right now would be a good time to make a few calls, and then I start to think about learning to use makeup and how maybe I could find some boyfriend who is not a total and complete fixer-upper and then my life would be totally great and I'd be happy all the time, and then I think about all the people I should have called back before I sat down to work, and how I should probably at least check in with my agent and tell him this great idea I have and see if he thinks it's a good idea, and see if he thinks I need orthodontia— if that is what he is actually thinking whenever we have lunch together. Then I think about someone I'm really annoyed with, or some financial problem that is driving me crazy, and decide that I must resolve this before I get down to today's work. So I become a dog with a chew toy, worrying it for a while, wrestling it to the ground, flinging it over my shoulder, chasing it, licking it, chewing it, flinging it back over my shoulder. I stop just short of actually barking. But all of this only takes somewhere between one and two minutes, so I haven't actually wasted that much time. Still, it leaves me winded. I go back to trying to breathe, slowly and calmly, and I finally notice the one-inch picture frame that I put on my desk to remind me of short assignments.

Copyright © BookheadEd Learning, LLC

Please note that excerpts and passages in the StudySync® library and this workbook are intended as touchstones to generate interest in an author's work. The excerpts and passages do not substitute for the reading of entire texts, and StudySync® strongly recommends that students seek out and purchase the whole literary or informational work in order to experience it as the author intended. Links to online resellers are available in our digital library. In addition, complete works may be ordered through an authorized reseller by filling out and returning to StudySync® the order form enclosed in this workbook.

3   It reminds me that all I have to do is to write down as much as I can see through a one-inch picture frame. This is all I have to bite off for the time being. All I am going to do right now, for example, is write that one paragraph that sets the story in my hometown, in the late fifties, when the trains were still running. I am going to paint a picture of it, in words, on my word processor[1]. Or all I am going to do is to describe the main character the very first time we meet her, when she first walks out the front door and onto the porch. I am not even going to describe the expression on her face when she first notices the blind dog sitting behind the wheel of her car—just what I can see through the one-inch picture frame, just one paragraph describing this woman, in the town where I grew up, the first time we **encounter** her.

4   E. L. Doctorow once said that "writing a novel is like driving a car at night. You can see only as far as your headlights, but you can make the whole trip that way." You don't have to see where you're going, you don't have to see your destination or everything you will pass along the way. You just have to see two or three feet ahead of you. This is right up there with the best advice about writing, or life, I have ever heard.

5   So after I've completely exhausted myself thinking about the people I most resent in the world, and my more arresting financial problems, and, of course, the orthodontia, I remember to pick up the one-inch picture frame and to figure out a one-inch piece of my story to tell, one small scene, one memory, one exchange. I also remember a story that I know I've told elsewhere but that over and over helps me to get a grip: thirty years ago my older brother, who was ten years old at the time, was trying to get a report on birds written that he'd had three months to write, which was due the next day. We were out at our family cabin in Bolinas, and he was at the kitchen table close to tears, surrounded by binder paper and pencils and unopened books on birds, **immobilized** by the hugeness of the task ahead. Then my father sat down beside him, put his arm around my brother's shoulder, and said, "Bird by bird, buddy. Just take it bird by bird."

6   I tell this story again because it usually makes a dent in the tremendous sense of being **overwhelmed** that my students experience. Sometimes it actually gives them hope, and hope, as Chesterton said, "is the power of being cheerful in circumstances that we know to be **desperate**." Writing can be a pretty desperate endeavor, because it is about some of our deepest needs: our need to be visible, to be heard, our need to make sense of our lives, to wake up and grow and belong. It is no wonder if we sometimes tend to take ourselves perhaps a bit too seriously.

---

1. **word processor** a standalone device or machine used for writing and printing written documents before the invention of the personal computer

Please note that excerpts and passages in the StudySync® library and this workbook are intended as touchstones to generate interest in an author's work. The excerpts and passages do not substitute for the reading of entire texts, and StudySync® strongly recommends that students seek out and purchase the whole literary or informational work in order to experience it as the author intended. Links to online resellers are available in our digital library. In addition, complete works may be ordered through an authorized reseller by filling out and returning to StudySync® the order form enclosed in this workbook.

Copyright © BookheadEd Learning, LLC

Excerpted from *Bird by Bird: Some Instructions on Writing and Life* by Anne Lamott, published by Anchor Books.

✏ WRITE

EXPLANATORY ESSAY: The author uses several examples of figurative language to describe her ongoing experience with anxiety. Identify three instances of figurative language, explain their meaning, and evaluate how effective these examples are in supporting the writer's thesis.

Please note that excerpts and passages in the StudySync® library and this workbook are intended as touchstones to generate interest in an author's work. The excerpts and passages do not substitute for the reading of entire texts, and StudySync® strongly recommends that students seek out and purchase the whole literary or informational work in order to experience it as the author intended. Links to online resellers are available in our digital library. In addition, complete works may be ordered through an authorized reseller by filling out and returning to StudySync® the order form enclosed in this workbook.

Copyright © BookheadEd Learning, LLC

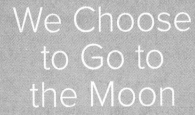

We Choose to Go to the Moon

ARGUMENTATIVE TEXT
John F. Kennedy
1962

Introduction

studysync ⓥ

After the Soviet Union's successful launch of *Sputnik* in October of 1957, the United States entered the Space Race, quickly forming the National Aeronautics and Space Administration (NASA) and working to launch its own satellites. Within five years, both the U.S. and U.S.S.R. had launched manned spacecraft. The Soviets initially soared ahead, putting the first man in space and successfully penetrating the Moon's atmosphere. Landing a man on the Moon was the most coveted prize of all, however, and President John F. Kennedy (1917–1963) was determined for America to accomplish it first. At Houston's Rice University, in September of 1962, he spoke of this quest before an audience of 35,000 people. His impassioned speech ignited the country, inspiring Americans everywhere to embrace the challenge of putting a man on the Moon. His impassioned speech ignited the country, inspiring Americans everywhere to embrace the challenge of putting a man on the Moon by highlighting America's spirit of determination and innovation.

"The greater our knowledge increases, the greater our ignorance unfolds."

Copyright © BookheadEd Learning, LLC

NOTES

Skill:
Author's Purpose
and Point of View

The president appeals to his audience with a repetitive assertion of the values of the place he is speaking in. This both sets the purpose for his speech, and emotionally flatters his audience.

1   We meet at a college noted for knowledge, in a city noted for progress, in a state noted for strength, and we stand in need of all three, for we meet in an hour of change and challenge, in a decade of hope and fear, in an age of both knowledge and ignorance. The greater our knowledge increases, the greater our ignorance unfolds.

2   Despite the striking fact that most of the scientists that the world has ever known are alive and working today, despite the fact that this Nation's own scientific manpower is doubling every 12 years in a rate of growth more than three times that of our population as a whole, despite that, the vast stretches of the unknown and the unanswered and the unfinished still far outstrip our collective comprehension. . .

3   Surely the opening **vistas** of space promise high costs and hardships, as well as high reward. So it is not surprising that some would have us stay where we are a little longer to rest, to wait. But this city of Houston, this state of Texas, this country of the United States, was not built by those who waited and rested and wished to look behind them. This country was conquered by those who moved forward—and so will space.

4   . . . [M]an, in his quest for knowledge and progress, is determined and cannot be deterred. The exploration of space will go ahead, whether we join in it or not, and it is one of the great adventures of all time, and no nation which expects to be the leader of other nations can expect to stay behind in this race for space.

5   Those who came before us made certain that this country rode the first waves of the industrial revolution, the first waves of modern invention, and the first wave of nuclear power, and this generation does not intend to **founder** in the backwash of the coming age of space. We mean to be a part of it—we mean to lead it. For the eyes of the world now look into space, to the Moon and to the planets beyond, and we have vowed that we shall not see it governed by a **hostile** flag of conquest, but by a banner of freedom and peace. We have vowed that we shall not see space filled with weapons of mass destruction, but with instruments of knowledge and understanding.

Please note that excerpts and passages in the StudySync® library and this workbook are intended as touchstones to generate interest in an author's work. The excerpts and passages do not substitute for the reading of entire texts, and StudySync® strongly recommends that students seek out and purchase the whole literary or informational work in order to experience it as the author intended. Links to online resellers are available in our digital library. In addition, complete works may be ordered through an authorized reseller by filling out and returning to StudySync® the order form enclosed in this workbook.

6   Yet the vows of this Nation can only be fulfilled if we in this Nation are first, and, therefore, we intend to be first. In short, our leadership in science and industry, our hopes for peace and security, our obligations to ourselves as well as others, all require us to make this effort, to solve these mysteries, to solve them for the good of all men, and to become the world's leading space-faring nation.

7   We set sail on this new sea because there is new knowledge to be gained, and new rights to be won, and they must be won and used for the progress of all people. For space science, like nuclear science and all technology, has no conscience of its own. Whether it will become a force for good or ill depends on man, and only if the United States occupies a position of pre-eminence can we help decide whether this new ocean will be a sea of peace or a new terrifying theater of war. . .

8   There is no strife, no prejudice, no national conflict in outer space as yet. Its hazards are hostile to us all. Its conquest deserves the best of all mankind, and its opportunity for peaceful cooperation many never come again. But why, some say, the Moon? Why choose this as our goal? And they may well ask why climb the highest mountain? Why, 35 years ago, fly the Atlantic? Why does Rice play Texas?

9   We choose to go to the Moon. We choose to go to the Moon in this decade and do the other things, not because they are easy, but because they are hard, because that goal will serve to organize and measure the best of our energies and skills, because that challenge is one that we are willing to accept, one we are unwilling to postpone, and one which we intend to win, and the others, too.

10   It is for these reasons that I regard the decision last year to shift our efforts in space from low to high gear as among the most important decisions that will be made during my incumbency in the office of the Presidency. . .

11   Within these last 19 months at least 45 satellites have circled the earth. Some 40 of them were "made in the United States of America" and they were far more sophisticated and supplied far more knowledge to the people of the world than those of the Soviet Union . . .

12   We have had our failures, but so have others, even if they do not admit them. And they may be less public.

13   To be sure, we are behind, and will be behind for some time in manned flight. But we do not intend to stay behind, and in this decade, we shall make up and move ahead.

Skill:
Arguments and Claims

The president builds on his previous argument by elaborating on why these ambitious goals and accepted realities are impactful and effective. The further this argument goes logically, the more effective it is.

Skill:
Rhetoric

In this passage I see ethos: he was President! He also uses pathos when he appeals to patriotism by talking about how good American satellites are. He uses logos when he says that being behind doesn't mean we can't catch up.

Please note that excerpts and passages in the StudySync® library and this workbook are intended as touchstones to generate interest in an author's work. The excerpts and passages do not substitute for the reading of entire texts, and StudySync® strongly recommends that students seek out and purchase the whole literary or informational work in order to experience it as the author intended. Links to online resellers are available in our digital library. In addition, complete works may be ordered through an authorized reseller by filling out and returning to StudySync® the order form enclosed in this workbook.

Copyright © BookheadEd Learning, LLC

NOTES

14 The growth of our science and education will be enriched by new knowledge of our universe and environment, by new techniques of learning and mapping and observation, by new tools and computers for industry, medicine, the home as well as the school. Technical institutions, such as Rice, will reap the harvest of these gains.

15 And finally, the space effort itself, while still in its infancy, has already created a great number of new companies, and tens of thousands of new jobs. . .

16 To be sure, all this costs us all a good deal of money. This year's space budget is three times what it was in January 1961, and it is greater than the space budget of the previous eight years combined. . .

17 But if I were to say, my fellow citizens, that we shall send to the Moon, 240,000 miles away from the control station in Houston, a giant rocket more than 300 feet tall, the length of this football field, made of new metal alloys, some of which have not yet been invented, capable of standing heat and stresses several times more than have ever been experienced, fitted together with a precision better than the finest watch, carrying all the equipment needed for propulsion, guidance, control, communications, food and survival, on an untried mission, to an unknown **celestial** body, and then return it safely to earth, re-entering the atmosphere at speeds of over 25,000 miles per hour, causing heat about half that of the temperature of the sun—almost as hot as it is here today—and do all this, and do it right, and do it first before this decade is out—then we must be bold. . .

Edwin "Buzz" Aldrin becomes the second man to walk on the moon, July 21, 1969

18 Many years ago the great British explorer George Mallory, who was to die on Mount Everest, was asked why did he want to climb it. He said, "Because it is there."

19 Well, space is there, and we're going to climb it, and the Moon and the planets are there, and new hopes for knowledge and peace are there. And, therefore, as we set sail we ask God's blessing on the most hazardous and dangerous and greatest adventure on which man has ever **embarked**.

Skill:
Author's Purpose
and Point of View

I imagine that, for the audience, who are living in a time before humans had explored space, this would have felt impossible but also very exciting.

Copyright © BookheadEd Learning, LLC

Please note that excerpts and passages in the StudySync® library and this workbook are intended as touchstones to generate interest in an author's work. The excerpts and passages do not substitute for the reading of entire texts, and StudySync® strongly recommends that students seek out and purchase the whole literary or informational work in order to experience it as the author intended. Links to online resellers are available in our digital library. In addition, complete works may be ordered through an authorized reseller by filling out and returning to StudySync® the order form enclosed in this workbook.

First Read

Read "We Choose to Go to the Moon." After you read, complete the Think Questions below.

 THINK QUESTIONS

1. According to President Kennedy, what are some of the drawbacks to space travel? Support your answer with evidence from paragraphs 3, 8, and 16.

2. Why does President Kennedy believe it is vital for the United States to be the leader in space travel? Support your answer with evidence from paragraphs 5 and 6.

3. President Kennedy refers to the Soviet Union by name only once in this excerpt. Yet he refers to them indirectly in paragraphs 5 and 13. Based on these indirect references, what can you infer about how Kennedy feels about the Soviet Union?

4. Use context to determine the meaning of the word **founder** as it is used in "We Choose to Go to the Moon." Write your definition of *founder* here and explain which context clues helped you determine its meaning.

5. Use context to determine the meaning of the word **embarked** as it is used in "We Choose to Go to the Moon." Then verify your definition by consulting a print or digital dictionary.

Copyright © BookheadEd Learning, LLC

Please note that excerpts and passages in the StudySync® library and this workbook are intended as touchstones to generate interest in an author's work. The excerpts and passages do not substitute for the reading of entire texts, and StudySync® strongly recommends that students seek out and purchase the whole literary or informational work in order to experience it as the author intended. Links to online resellers are available in our digital library. In addition, complete works may be ordered through an authorized reseller by filling out and returning to StudySync® the order form enclosed in this workbook.

Reading & Writing Companion

65

Skill:
Author's Purpose and Point of View

Use the Checklist to analyze Author's Purpose and Point of View in "We Choose to Go to the Moon." Refer to the sample student annotations about Author's Purpose and Point of View in the text.

••• CHECKLIST FOR AUTHOR'S PURPOSE AND POINT OF VIEW

In order to identify author or speaker's purpose and point of view, note the following:

- ✓ whether the writer is attempting to establish trust by citing his or her experience or education

- ✓ whether the evidence the author or speaker provides is convincing and the argument or position is logical

- ✓ what words and phrases the author or speaker uses to appeal to emotions

- ✓ the author or speaker's use of rhetoric, or the art of speaking and writing persuasively, such as the use of repetition to drive home a point, as well as allusion and alliteration

- ✓ the author or speaker's use of rhetoric to contribute to the power, persuasiveness, or beauty of the text

To determine the author or speaker's purpose and point of view, consider the following questions:

- ✓ How does the author or speaker try to convince me that he or she has something valid and important for me to read?

- ✓ What words or phrases express emotion or invite an emotional response? How or why are they effective or ineffective?

- ✓ What words and phrases contribute to the power, persuasiveness, or beauty of the text? Is the author or speaker's use of rhetoric successful? Why or why not?

Copyright © BookheadEd Learning, LLC

Please note that excerpts and passages in the StudySync® library and this workbook are intended as touchstones to generate interest in an author's work. The excerpts and passages do not substitute for the reading of entire texts, and StudySync® strongly recommends that students seek out and purchase the whole literary or informational work in order to experience it as the author intended. Links to online resellers are available in our digital library. In addition, complete works may be ordered through an authorized reseller by filling out and returning to StudySync® the order form enclosed in this workbook.

Skill:
Author's Purpose and
Point of View

Reread paragraphs 3 and 4 of "We Choose to Go to the Moon." Then, using the Checklist on the previous page, answer the multiple-choice questions below.

⟳ YOUR TURN

1. Which of the following sentences from the speech is the best statement of president Kennedy's purpose?

   ○ A. "This country was conquered by those who moved forward—and so will space."

   ○ B. ". . . [M]an, in his quest for knowledge and progress, is determined and cannot be deterred."

   ○ C. "So it is not surprising that some would have us stay where we are a little longer to rest, to wait."

   ○ D. "But this city of Houston, this state of Texas, this country of the United States, was not built by those who waited and rested and wished to look behind them."

2. Which of the following sentences is the best example of the president appealing to his audience's emotions?

   ○ A. "This country was conquered by those who moved forward—and so will space."

   ○ B. "But this city of Houston, this state of Texas, this country of the United States, was not built by those who waited and rested and wished to look behind them."

   ○ C. "The exploration of space will go ahead, whether we join in it or not, and it is one of the great adventures of all time, and no nation which expects to be the leader of other nations can expect to stay behind in this race for space."

   ○ D. "Surely the opening **vistas** of space promise high costs and hardships, as well as high reward."

3. Why is the emotional appeal in Question 2 likely to be effective?

   ○ A. In this appeal, the president appeals to the audience's hopes and fears.

   ○ B. In this appeal, the president makes historical references.

   ○ C. In this appeal, the president speaks indirectly to the Soviet Union.

   ○ D. In this appeal, the president speaks directly to the pride of Houston, Texas, and the entire country.

Copyright © BookheadEd Learning, LLC

Please note that excerpts and passages in the StudySync® library and this workbook are intended as touchstones to generate interest in an author's work. The excerpts and passages do not substitute for the reading of entire texts, and StudySync® strongly recommends that students seek out and purchase the whole literary or informational work in order to experience it as the author intended. Links to online resellers are available in our digital library. In addition, complete works may be ordered through an authorized reseller by filling out and returning to StudySync® the order form enclosed in this workbook.

Reading & Writing
Companion

67

Skill:
Rhetoric

Use the Checklist to analyze Rhetoric in "We Choose to Go to the Moon." Refer to the sample student annotations about Rhetoric in the text.

••• CHECKLIST FOR RHETORIC

In order to identify the rhetorical appeals in a text, note the following:

✓ the purpose of the text

✓ the way in which a writer phrases, or constructs, what he or she wants to say

✓ details and statements that identify the author or speaker's point of view or purpose

To identify how the author or speaker uses rhetorical appeals, look for:

✓ the three elements of persuasion as defined by Aristotle: ethos, pathos, and logos. Ethos relies on the authority or credibility of the person making the argument to try to convince an audience. Pathos is an appeal to emotion. Logos is an appeal to reason or logic.

✓ words that appeal to the senses or emotions and can create a vivid picture in the minds of readers and listeners, and persuade them to accept a specific point of view

✓ a specific style, such as the use of assonance or the repetition of certain words can be used to create catchphrases, something that can be widely or repeatedly used and is easily remembered

✓ when the author or speaker's use of rhetorical appeal is particularly effective

In order to identify the rhetorical appeals in a text, note the following:

✓ Which rhetorical appeals can you identify in the text?

✓ How does this writer or speaker use rhetorical devices or appeals to persuade an audience?

✓ Do the rhetorical devices or appeals work to make the argument or position sound? Why or why not?

✓ How does the use of rhetorical devices or appeals affect the way the text is read and understood?

✓ In what way are the rhetorical devices particularly effective?

Copyright © BookheadEd Learning, LLC

Please note that excerpts and passages in the StudySync® library and this workbook are intended as touchstones to generate interest in an author's work. The excerpts and passages do not substitute for the reading of entire texts, and StudySync® strongly recommends that students seek out and purchase the whole literary or informational work in order to experience it as the author intended. Links to online resellers are available in our digital library. In addition, complete works may be ordered through an authorized reseller by filling out and returning to StudySync® the order form enclosed in this workbook.

Skill:
Rhetoric

Reread paragraphs 17–19 of "We Choose to Go to the Moon." Then, using the Checklist on the previous page, answer the multiple-choice questions below.

⟳ YOUR TURN

1. The use of word repetition in paragraph 17 is most obvious in the phrase—

   ○ A. "Well, space is there, and we're going to climb it, and the Moon and the planets are there."
   ○ B. "with a precision better than the finest watch."
   ○ C. "propulsion, guidance, control, communications, food and survival."
   ○ D. "and do all this, and do it right, and do it first."

2. Paragraph 19 is mostly an example of what form of rhetorical appeal:

   ○ A. ethos
   ○ B. logos
   ○ C. pathos
   ○ D. word repetition

3. The final sentence of paragraph 19 is persuasive largely because—

   ○ A. it includes logical fallacies, such as the claim that boats can sail into space.
   ○ B. Kennedy was one of the world's leading experts on space science.
   ○ C. it appeals to emotion by describing the wonders of a trip to the Moon.
   ○ D. it appeals to reason by giving facts and figures about the trip to the Moon.

Copyright © BookheadEd Learning, LLC

Please note that excerpts and passages in the StudySync® library and this workbook are intended as touchstones to generate interest in an author's work. The excerpts and passages do not substitute for the reading of entire texts, and StudySync® strongly recommends that students seek out and purchase the whole literary or informational work in order to experience it as the author intended. Links to online resellers are available in our digital library. In addition, complete works may be ordered through an authorized reseller by filling out and returning to StudySync® the order form enclosed in this workbook.

Reading & Writing Companion   69

Skill:
Arguments and Claims

Use the Checklist to analyze Arguments and Claims in "We Choose to Go to the Moon." Refer to the sample student annotations about Arguments and Claims in the text.

••• CHECKLIST FOR ARGUMENTS AND CLAIMS

In order to delineate the premises, purposes, and arguments in works of public advocacy, note the following:

✓ in works of public advocacy, an individual or group tries to influence or support a cause or policy

✓ the premise, or the basis of the proposal the individual or group makes, must be based on logical reasoning

✓ isolate the premise in a work of public advocacy

✓ identify the purpose of the text and the position the writer takes

✓ determine whether the premise is based on logical reasoning

To evaluate the premises, purposes, and arguments in works of public advocacy, consider the following questions:

✓ What position does the writer take?

✓ How does the writer use logical reasoning to support his or her position?

✓ In a work of public advocacy, how does the individual or group try to influence or support a cause or policy?

Copyright © BookheadEd Learning, LLC

Please note that excerpts and passages in the StudySync® library and this workbook are intended as touchstones to generate interest in an author's work. The excerpts and passages do not substitute for the reading of entire texts, and StudySync® strongly recommends that students seek out and purchase the whole literary or informational work in order to experience it as the author intended. Links to online resellers are available in our digital library. In addition, complete works may be ordered through an authorized reseller by filling out and returning to StudySync® the order form enclosed in this workbook.

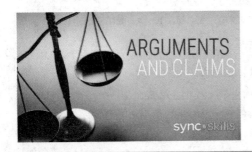

Skill:
Arguments and Claims

Reread paragraphs 11–14 of "We Choose to Go to the Moon." Then, using the Checklist on the previous page, answer the multiple-choice questions below.

⟳ YOUR TURN

1. What is the most likely reason the president shares that "Within these last 19 months at least 45 satellites have circled the earth. Some 40 of them were 'made in the United States of America'"?

   ○ A. He shares this timeline and numbers to create anxiety.

   ○ B. He shares this timeline and numbers to give the audience a logical premise and reason to hope.

   ○ C. He shares this timeline and numbers to create additional jobs for Americans.

   ○ D. He shares this timeline and numbers to give Americans another reason to compete with the Soviet Union.

2. Why does the president share the failures and challenges that we will face?

   ○ A. The president shares the failures and challenges because the perils of space exploration were largely unknown.

   ○ B. The president shares the failures and challenges because he wants those involved in the space program to admit their mistakes.

   ○ C. The president shares the failures and challenges because a real description will prevent future failures.

   ○ D. The president shares the failures and challenges because a real description of the situation acknowledges the challenges ahead, but also provides an argument for action.

Copyright © BookheadEd Learning, LLC

Please note that excerpts and passages in the StudySync® library and this workbook are intended as touchstones to generate interest in an author's work. The excerpts and passages do not substitute for the reading of entire texts, and StudySync® strongly recommends that students seek out and purchase the whole literary or informational work in order to experience it as the author intended. Links to online resellers are available in our digital library. In addition, complete works may be ordered through an authorized reseller by filling out and returning to StudySync® the order form enclosed in this workbook.

Reading & Writing Companion   **71**

3. Which of the following sentences best supports the president's argument that the benefits of the space program will be felt by his audience?

○ A. "Technical institutions, such as Rice, will reap the harvest of these gains."

○ B. "Some 40 of them were "made in the United States of America" and they were far more sophisticated and supplied far more knowledge to the people of the world than those of the Soviet Union. . . "

○ C. "To be sure, we are behind, and will be behind for some time in manned flight. But we do not intend to stay behind, and in this decade, we shall make up and move ahead."

○ D. "We have had our failures, but so have others, even if they do not admit them. And they may be less public."

Copyright © BookheadEd Learning, LLC

Please note that excerpts and passages in the StudySync® library and this workbook are intended as touchstones to generate interest in an author's work. The excerpts and passages do not substitute for the reading of entire texts, and StudySync® strongly recommends that students seek out and purchase the whole literary or informational work in order to experience it as the author intended. Links to online resellers are available in our digital library. In addition, complete works may be ordered through an authorized reseller by filling out and returning to StudySync® the order form enclosed in this workbook.

Close Read

Reread "We Choose to Go to the Moon." As you reread, complete the Skills Focus questions below. Then use your answers and annotations from the questions to help you complete the Write activity.

⊚ SKILLS FOCUS

1. Reread paragraph 5. What does the president reveal is part of his purpose in this paragraph? What emotion would this appeal to in his audience? Do you think it's effective?

2. Highlight and annotate two examples in which the president uses pathos to appeal to the audience's emotions. Explain whether you find these appeals persuasive and why.

3. Reread the second half of the speech. Find a sentence that appeals to the audience's sense of reason or logic. Explain why Kennedy might have chosen to use this rhetorical device, and whether or not it is effective.

4. In several key moments of this speech, the president chooses to use timelines, numbers, and statistics. Highlight two examples of this, and in your annotation explain why these numbers are useful to the president's argument. How would these numbers influence his audience?

5. In this speech, president Kennedy argues for a goal that will require tons of energy, effort, and resources. What is the future that the president is envisioning? Why is it a motivating future, if it can be attained? Why does Kennedy need to convince his audience of the possibility of this future? Remember to use textual evidence in your response

✏ WRITE

RHETORICAL ANALYSIS: Examine the reasons President Kennedy lists for wanting to **cultivate** the space program and send Americans to the Moon by the end of the 1960s. Based on his speech, what do you think motivates him? Do you find his arguments and use of rhetoric persuasive? Use evidence from the text to support your answer.

Please note that excerpts and passages in the StudySync® library and this workbook are intended as touchstones to generate interest in an author's work. The excerpts and passages do not substitute for the reading of entire texts, and StudySync® strongly recommends that students seek out and purchase the whole literary or informational work in order to experience it as the author intended. Links to online resellers are available in our digital library. In addition, complete works may be ordered through an authorized reseller by filling out and returning to StudySync® the order form enclosed in this workbook.

Reading & Writing Companion   73

Copyright © BookheadEd Learning, LLC

Blast: The Write Stuff

How do you tell the story of who you are and who you want to become?

Copyright © Bookheaded Learning, LLC

NOTES

ⓘ BACKGROUND

Listen to the What's Next podcast associated with this Blast in your digital account.

When you finally click "Submit" and send your personal statement into the abyss of an online application portal, where does it go?

Anxious college applicants might imagine their essays go to a panel of harsh, judgmental, easily bored professors. However, this isn't accurate, according to Will Dix, a longtime college admissions counselor. "For a lot of admission people, it's kind of the dessert of a college application," says Dix. "We want to like your essay. We're not there to make corrections with red pens and so on. We do notice whether you're writing well or not, but we want to hear your voice, and that's always the primary thing."

So, how do you make sure your voice shines through in a short essay? First, pick a topic that actually matters to you. The four years you spent playing baseball might sound impressive, but unless you truly care about the game, the essay will fall flat. Rachel Toor, a creative writing professor at Eastern Washington University, says unconventional topics often make for great essays. "Write about whatever keeps you up at night," Toor writes. "That might be cars, or coffee. It might be your favorite book or the Pythagorean theorem."

Second, use anecdotes to tell a compelling story. Instead of writing a broad overview of your life, pick a moment to zoom in on. Be sure to pick a moment that symbolizes what you want to convey. "Most students think of their college

Reading & Writing Companion

Please note that excerpts and passages in the StudySync® library and this workbook are intended as touchstones to generate interest in an author's work. The excerpts and passages do not substitute for the reading of entire texts, and StudySync® strongly recommends that students seek out and purchase the whole literary or informational work in order to experience it as the author intended. Links to online resellers are available in our digital library. In addition, complete works may be ordered through an authorized reseller by filling out and returning to StudySync® the order form enclosed in this workbook.

essay as a major motion picture. They feel they need to cover the highlights (or, too often, the tragedies) of years of experience," Parke Muth, senior assistant dean and director of international admissions at the University of Virginia, tells U.S. News and World Report "The problem is that to write about a life in 500 words will result in a cinematic long shot . . . I tell students it is not a movie they are making but a Nike ad." Muth explains that the best essays make it easy to "hear, see, touch, taste, and sometimes even smell" the student's world.

Finally, write your essay well. Use vibrant words, clear sentence structure and correct spelling, grammar and punctuation. Many experts recommend having one or two teachers or trusted family members read over your essay. They can help you revise and edit.

In the end, Toor says, "most essays are typical. Many are boring. Some are just plain bad. But occasionally one will make an admissions officer tear down the hallway to find a colleague to whom she can say, 'You have to read what this Math Olympiad girl said about Hamlet.' Your goal is to write an essay that makes someone fall in love with you."

So, what do you think? How do you show who you are and what makes you special in just a few hundred words? How will you make your essay shine? How do you tell the story of who you are and who you want to become?

NUMBER CRUNCH

650

QUIKPOLL

What are you most likely to write your college essay about?

- ☐ Academics or activities at school
- ☐ My family or childhood
- ☐ My friends or social life outside of school
- ☐ An experience that changed the way I see the world
- ☐ Something else

Copyright © BookheadEd Learning, LLC

Please note that excerpts and passages in the StudySync® library and this workbook are intended as touchstones to generate interest in an author's work. The excerpts and passages do not substitute for the reading of entire texts, and StudySync® strongly recommends that students seek out and purchase the whole literary or informational work in order to experience it as the author intended. Links to online resellers are available in our digital library. In addition, complete works may be ordered through an authorized reseller by filling out and returning to StudySync® the order form enclosed in this workbook.

Reading & Writing Companion   75

✸ CREATE YOUR BLAST

How do you tell the story of who you are and who you want to become?

_____

_____

_____

_____

Please note that excerpts and passages in the StudySync® library and this workbook are intended as touchstones to generate interest in an author's work. The excerpts and passages do not substitute for the reading of entire texts, and StudySync® strongly recommends that students seek out and purchase the whole literary or informational work in order to experience it as the author intended. Links to online resellers are available in our digital library. In addition, complete works may be ordered through an authorized reseller by filling out and returning to StudySync® the order form enclosed in this workbook.

Copyright © BookheadEd Learning, LLC

Blast: Narrowing the Field

What qualities do you look for in a college?

Copyright © BookheadEd Learning, LLC

ℹ BACKGROUND

Listen to the What's Next podcast associated with this Blast in your digital account.

What is the longest amount of time you have spent preparing for something? Maybe you spent a month learning a language for a trip out of the country. Maybe you spent weeks planning for a family trip. Both situations involve a fair amount of patience and effort. The desired payoff is having an experience that is worth every penny. You will need those same skills if you plan on applying to colleges.

The college application process requires patience and effort on a much broader scale. Finding the right fit in a college requires thinking about many different factors. It also requires thinking about many different schools. There are about 3,000 four-year colleges and universities in the United States, not including the estimated 1,600 two-year institutions, according to the National Center for Education Statistics. You may want to approach your search with specific requirements. Are there certain regions of the country you would prefer to live in? Do you like the idea of a small liberal arts school or a large public university? These questions can narrow your search significantly. Online tools, such as the U.S. Department of Education's College Scorecard, account for a wide range of preferences in college searches.

There is not one single college characteristic that is universally important to every college applicant. Martha O'Connell is the executive director of college advisory organization Colleges That Change Lives. She says that you need to ask yourself four main questions about your reasons for going to college

---

Please note that excerpts and passages in the StudySync® library and this workbook are intended as touchstones to generate interest in an author's work. The excerpts and passages do not substitute for the reading of entire texts, and StudySync® strongly recommends that students seek out and purchase the whole literary or informational work in order to experience it as the author intended. Links to online resellers are available in our digital library. In addition, complete works may be ordered through an authorized reseller by filling out and returning to StudySync® the order form enclosed in this workbook.

before you start your search. "Why, really, are you going? What are your abilities and strengths? What are your weaknesses," O'Connell asked in NPR. "What do you want out of life — something tangible or intangible?"

Your ideal college lifestyle is an important step in college decisions. How much will it cost to head far from home? What does the campus offer? Take a look at internship opportunities, entertainment options and the availability of public transportation. It's also valuable to check and see if there are established clubs or organizations that you'd want to participate in at different universities.

Accounting for a college lifestyle that works for you is vital, but so is picking a school with the right program and potential major. These choices will impact your life long after graduation. However, many high schoolers aren't ready to commit to a career track right away. Roughly 30 percent of college students change their major at least once before graduation, according to a 2017 study by the Department of Education. If you feel unsure about your dream job, then do not stress about how one business school stacks up against another. But if you do have a good idea of what you want to do, you can balance the benefits that come with attending a university that has a strong reputation in a certain department versus the university's other qualities.

For some students, the average annual cost of college is the most weighty and important factor. O'Connell recommends not ruling any university based on the sticker price of tuition. "Online resources, as well as financial aid workshops sponsored by high schools in local communities, are widely available to get you started," O'Connell says. "Investigate early and ask for help." Look for scholarships and grants that prospective schools offer, in-state versus out-of-state tuition, and the cost of living in different areas of the country.

Finally, as hard as it might be, try not to latch too strongly onto a dream school. *The Atlantic* analyzed a 2015 study published in the journal Contemporary Economic Policy about whether the prestige of a degree really helps students make more money. Its conclusion was that "for certain majors, going to a top-tier institution is invaluable. But for many career paths, it just doesn't matter where a person got his or her education."

What do you think? How do you research colleges? Which colleges are you interested in? What qualities do you look for in college?

NUMBER CRUNCH

40%

Copyright © BookheadEd Learning, LLC

Please note that excerpts and passages in the StudySync® library and this workbook are intended as touchstones to generate interest in an author's work. The excerpts and passages do not substitute for the reading of entire texts, and StudySync® strongly recommends that students seek out and purchase the whole literary or informational work in order to experience it as the author intended. Links to online resellers are available in our digital library. In addition, complete works may be ordered through an authorized reseller by filling out and returning to StudySync® the order form enclosed in this workbook.

◕ QUIKPOLL

How important are school sports at a potential college?

☐ Very important. I love sports, and I'm interested in schools with strong sports programs.

☐ Important. I'd like to go to games in college, but I'm not the biggest sports fan.

☐ Slightly important. I'd go to sports games, but I wouldn't mind going to a school without strong sports.

☐ Not important. I don't care about going to a college with school sports.

✳ CREATE YOUR BLAST

What qualities do you look for in a college?

_____

_____

_____

_____

Copyright © BookheadEd Learning, LLC

Please note that excerpts and passages in the StudySync® library and this workbook are intended as touchstones to generate interest in an author's work. The excerpts and passages do not substitute for the reading of entire texts, and StudySync® strongly recommends that students seek out and purchase the whole literary or informational work in order to experience it as the author intended. Links to online resellers are available in our digital library. In addition, complete works may be ordered through an authorized reseller by filling out and returning to StudySync® the order form enclosed in this workbook.

Blast: Filling in the Blanks

How can you best represent yourself in an application?

Copyright © BookheadEd Learning, LLC

NOTES

ⓘ BACKGROUND

Listen to the What's Next podcast associated with this Blast in your digital account.

One of the most exciting and nerve-wracking parts of graduating high school is figuring out what, exactly, comes next. By the time graduation comes, you have likely had many different experiences. You might have tried out for a sports team, a role in a play, or a leadership position in a club.

All of your experiences in school — and outside of school — are all important preparations for college and job applications. Each type of application has unique challenges. However, there are common tips that can help you stand out, no matter which path you choose to take.

You should feel fully comfortable with your background and your body of work before the application process starts, according to Diane Anci, the dean of admissions at Kenyon College. This can boost your confidence. "Knowing who you are provides a protective armor in a process that can be overwhelming," Anci says. "Not only are you inundated with communication from the colleges, everyone you know has an opinion of what is a good college and what is not, and they feel very free to express it."

It might be tempting to throw a laundry list of extracurriculars onto your application, but it can be more beneficial to hone in on the things you are most passionate about, or those skills that are most applicable to the specific college or job. Stuart Schmill is the dean of admissions at the Massachusetts

Please note that excerpts and passages in the StudySync® library and this workbook are intended as touchstones to generate interest in an author's work. The excerpts and passages do not substitute for the reading of entire texts, and StudySync® strongly recommends that students seek out and purchase the whole literary or informational work in order to experience it as the author intended. Links to online resellers are available in our digital library. In addition, complete works may be ordered through an authorized reseller by filling out and returning to StudySync® the order form enclosed in this workbook.

Institute of Technology. He says that selective colleges, especially, "want students who prioritize quality over quantity."

You can also make an impression and best represent yourself by personalizing your application for each college and job you are interested in. Jessica Yeager is a graduate of the Massachusetts Institute of Technology and Harvard University. She says that general responses in an essay or cover letter are not exciting to admissions officers. For colleges, she recommends "doing deep research, visiting campuses if you can, and trying to connect with professors or coaches," she said. "Weave all this information into your supplemental essays."

Supplemental essays or responses can highlight aspects of your personality or experience that do not shine through in the rest of your application. Stephen Farmer is the executive vice chancellor and provost at the University of North Carolina. He provided essay-writing advice to The New York Times. "My advice to students is to first show your essay to a friend and ask, 'Can you hear my voice in this? Could you pick my essay from a stack of 200?' The essay doesn't have to be about something life-changing or confessional," Farmer said. "Smaller topics, written well, almost always work best."

Finally, make sure that you take your time with your application. Yale University's admissions office also recommends getting constructive feedback from those you trust. "Share your essays with at least one or two people who know you well — such as a parent, teacher, counselor, or friend — and ask for feedback," the official admissions website says. A simple error can invalidate an otherwise superb application.

It is also important to remember to not get upset over rejected applications. You are not a failure if you do not get accepted to a certain school or job. Swarthmore College, for instance, rejected former President Barack Obama — and he transferred from a liberal arts college to an Ivy League university for his junior year. On average, a corporate opening leads to roughly 250 applications, according to job search website Glassdoor. Only four to six people are called in for interviews for that one position. The application process can be competitive and stressful. However, it will be worth it when you find the right fit. But don't take rejection too much to heart.

What do you think? Who do you trust to proofread your applications? Which of your life experiences are most important to highlight on your applications? How can you best represent yourself in an application?

NUMBER CRUNCH

2.9

Copyright © BookheadEd Learning, LLC

Please note that excerpts and passages in the StudySync® library and this workbook are intended as touchstones to generate interest in an author's work. The excerpts and passages do not substitute for the reading of entire texts, and StudySync® strongly recommends that students seek out and purchase the whole literary or informational work in order to experience it as the author intended. Links to online resellers are available in our digital library. In addition, complete works may be ordered through an authorized reseller by filling out and returning to StudySync® the order form enclosed in this workbook.

Reading & Writing Companion   81

NOTES

QUIKPOLL

Do you think the most interesting thing about you would best show your potential in the field of STEM, the Humanities, Business, or Education?

☐ I think the most interesting thing about me would show my potential in the field of STEM.

☐ I think the most interesting thing about me would show my potential in the field of the Humanities.

☐ I think the most interesting thing about me would show my potential in the field of Business.

☐ I think the most interesting thing about me would show my potential in the field of Education.

✹ CREATE YOUR BLAST

How can you best represent yourself in an application?

_____

_____

_____

_____

Copyright © BookheadEd Learning, LLC

Please note that excerpts and passages in the StudySync® library and this workbook are intended as touchstones to generate interest in an author's work. The excerpts and passages do not substitute for the reading of entire texts, and StudySync® strongly recommends that students seek out and purchase the whole literary or informational work in order to experience it as the author intended. Links to online resellers are available in our digital library. In addition, complete works may be ordered through an authorized reseller by filling out and returning to StudySync® the order form enclosed in this workbook.

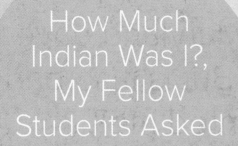

How Much Indian Was I?, My Fellow Students Asked

INFORMATIONAL TEXT
Elissa Washuta
2013

Introduction

Elissa Washuta is a lecturer at the University of Washington and teaches creative writing at the Institute of American Indian Arts. Her writings, primarily autobiographical essays and memoirs, include the Washington State Book Award finalist *My Body Is a Book of Rules*. In her short essay "How Much Indian Was I?, My Fellow Students Asked," Washuta, a nearly perfect student, receives a prestigious scholarship. The resulting journey to reconcile her success with her status as a Cowlitz tribe member is an exploration of race, culture, and identity in

"I'll never know why Maryland gave me a full scholarship. But is it so bad to think they wanted me?"

1   I came into my own as a Native American woman in high school. My skin being on the fair side of plain Yoplait, I **designated** my dark-brown hair as the body part that would legitimize me, letting its split ends shoot for my waist. The U.S. Census Bureau reported that in 2000, three Native Americans lived in Liberty Township, N.J.: my mom, my brother, and me, all enrolled members of the Cowlitz tribe.

2   In early 2003, I was a high-school senior. My only grade below an A was in gym class; on my report card, next to the B, the gym teacher wrote, "Works to ability." After nearly 13 years of academic perfectionism, I finally got a glimpse of the payoff when the University of Maryland at College Park sent me a letter inviting me to interview for a scholarship.

3   Inside the honors building I immediately noticed all the dark skin in the waiting room. I sat on the couch between my parents, wondering whether I should have worn some dream-catcher[1] earrings. My letter had said that this was an interview for a merit scholarship, with no mention of diversity. I worried that the interviewers were going to quiz me about my favorite Indian ceremonies. If they wanted me to speak in my native tongue, I would have to make something up on the spot. There was a lot of money on the line.

4   That day I wondered, what was so special about me that the adults would want to hand me what amounted to a sack filled with money? Not my poems, or my miniature clay sculptures of the members of Nirvana, or my gleaming transcripts. There were probably plenty of kids in the room who knew how to use their graphing calculators for purposes other than playing Tetris.

5   The interviewers greeted me with smiles. They asked about our drive from New Jersey and what I'd been reading. I talked about a book about Pine Ridge Reservation and my desire to work in Indian country. I told the nodding adults all about poverty, tradition, alcohol, and loss.

6   An ancient people in southwest Washington, the Cowlitz tribe maintains vibrant cultural practices and social and conservation programs despite its

---

1. **dream-catcher** a handmade item of spiritual significance in some Native American cultures, typically featuring a web or net woven into a willow hoop and adorned with feathers or beads

Copyright © BookheadEd Learning, LLC

Please note that excerpts and passages in the StudySync® library and this workbook are intended as touchstones to generate interest in an author's work. The excerpts and passages do not substitute for the reading of entire texts, and StudySync® strongly recommends that students seek out and purchase the whole literary or informational work in order to experience it as the author intended. Links to online resellers are available in our digital library. In addition, complete works may be ordered through an authorized reseller by filling out and returning to StudySync® the order form enclosed in this workbook.

lack of a reservation land base. My Cowlitz mom, who had lived in the Columbia River Gorge her whole life, met my East Coast dad in college in Seattle, and afterward they moved to New Jersey.

7   I didn't know how to talk about the histories embedded in my bones: the damming of our language that coincided with the damming of the Columbia River, my wordless conversations with the towering **petroglyph** woman by the water, my belly's swell that my mother told me was an Indian thing while I battled it with Weight Watchers point counts. I thought that if I spoke the truth, they would think all the Indianness had evaporated from my family line, leaving me pale and dry. So I said, "I want to do something for my people," and two weeks later, I received a thin letter thick with the promise of more money than I could imagine: four years of tuition, room, board, and books.

8   Not long after I hung my bell-bottom jeans and shower tote in my cinderblock closet, I told the kids on my floor of the honors dorm that in order to keep my scholarship, I'd have to obsess over every grade point. That money never went to white kids, they said, so I must be an undercover genius. I'm not all white, I said. What was my SAT score, they wanted to know. My GPA? Extracurriculars? How much Indian was I? The first thing I learned in college was that white boys don't care if you're legitimately Indian if they think you robbed them of $100,000 in scholarship money that they'd earned holding a tuba for countless hours on a high-school football field.

9   I threw myself into super-Indianness, taking both of the Native-studies courses offered by the university's **anthropology** department. I participated in a summer internship program for Native students and scored a part-time job in tribal relations with the U.S. Department of Agriculture. I graduated with a 4.0 GPA. If the university had wanted to reel in an Indian who could bring the numbers, I figured they had gotten what they paid for, as long as I became the Indian I had promised they were getting.

10 I didn't take any time off before shipping myself to Seattle for graduate school in creative writing at the University of Washington. The master's program offered me no teaching assistantship, and I told the program director I couldn't sign on unless the price tag was slashed. She came through with a university program committed to serving underrepresented graduate students. After I sent over a photocopy of my tribal card to add to the application, the grant program awarded me a generous partial scholarship. Creative-writing programs are notorious for the feelings of resentment that brew when students feel like a bunch of blood-hungry dogs made to scrap over funds granted on the basis of artistic **prowess**, but my colleagues were supportive of my scholarship.

11 In my application essay, I said that part of Washington's allure was its proximity to my tribe. I meant it. In the five years I have been at Washington, I have been attending Cowlitz general-council meetings and learning to participate. During

Copyright © BookheadEd Learning, LLC

Please note that excerpts and passages in the StudySync® library and this workbook are intended as touchstones to generate interest in an author's work. The excerpts and passages do not substitute for the reading of entire texts, and StudySync® strongly recommends that students seek out and purchase the whole literary or informational work in order to experience it as the author intended. Links to online resellers are available in our digital library. In addition, complete works may be ordered through an authorized reseller by filling out and returning to StudySync® the order form enclosed in this workbook.

Reading & Writing Companion

85

NOTES

my second year, I was a graduate assistant for the department of American Indian studies, and I now serve as the undergraduate adviser. I also teach classes that focus on Native literature and film representations of Natives.

12   I'd love to see more Native students at Washington and elsewhere. Native people deserve to be educated in spite of the extraordinary challenges many face because of uniquely broken educational systems wrapped up in the mangled trust relationship that sets Indian identity apart from other racial or ethnic distinctions. Native people hold an elemental piece of this nation's life story, and universities will suffer without an indigenous presence.

13   Those interviewers back at Maryland would be happy with my academic career, I think. My work these days comes with a clear mission: to help the students I teach learn who we are and who we are not, and to help them— especially those who were least prepared because of their backgrounds— navigate the academic maze. I wish my students could stop worrying about money—who's getting it, why, and how they're going to get some of their own—so they can focus on learning to write killer essays and getting smarter than they ever thought possible.

14   I'll never know why Maryland gave me a full scholarship. But is it so bad to think they wanted me? As my gym teacher noticed, I "work to ability." I pull out all the stops in every class. Perhaps the interviewers sensed my yearning to go for broke and to stuff every synapse with academic pleasures.

15   From my family and Native communities, I have learned about the gifting tradition. In our culture, accepting a gift with grace and giving meaningful gifts are skills more important, and more difficult to **cultivate**, than learning to graph calculus problems. So I have stopped apologizing for the gifts I receive. I accept them. And now I have my own gifting to do.

Used with permission of The Chronicle of Higher Education Copyright © 2017. All rights reserved.

Copyright © BookheadEd Learning, LLC

✏ **WRITE**

PERSONAL RESPONSE: Today, many people are turning to online services such as Ancestry.com to discover their backgrounds. Do you think that knowing your ethnic makeup and cultural heritage is important in order to forge your identity? Why or why not? Write an essay of 300 or more words arguing your position. Use details from this selection and from your own life to develop your ideas.

Please note that excerpts and passages in the StudySync® library and this workbook are intended as touchstones to generate interest in an author's work. The excerpts and passages do not substitute for the reading of entire texts, and StudySync® strongly recommends that students seek out and purchase the whole literary or informational work in order to experience it as the author intended. Links to online resellers are available in our digital library. In addition, complete works may be ordered through an authorized reseller by filling out and returning to StudySync® the order form enclosed in this workbook.

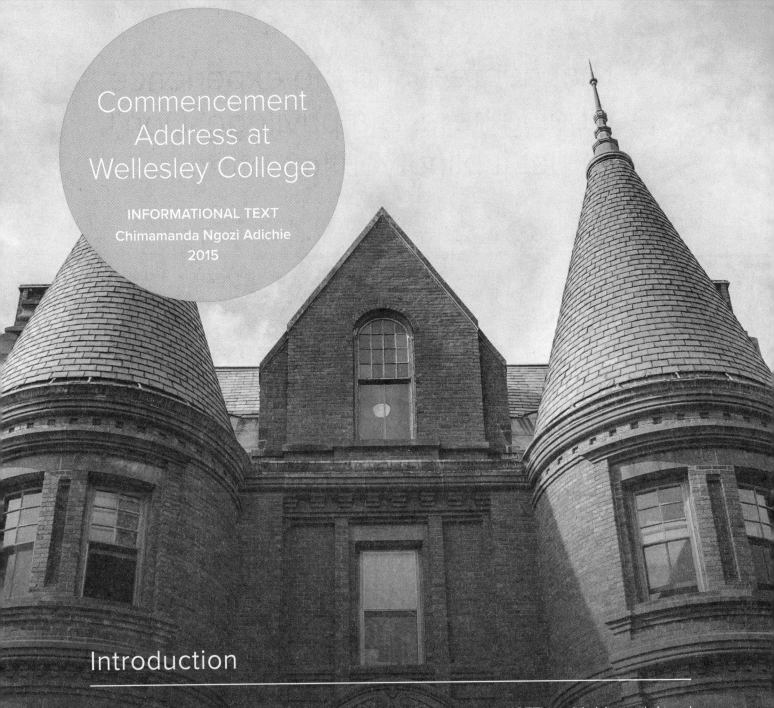

Commencement Address at Wellesley College

INFORMATIONAL TEXT
Chimamanda Ngozi Adichie
2015

Introduction

Nigerian-born author Chimamanda Ngozi Adichie (b. 1977) is a highly acclaimed novelist, short-story writer, and critic whose advocacy on behalf of gender equality was first introduced to mass audiences in the 2013 Beyoncé song "Flawless," which samples an Adichie speech entitled "We Should All Be Feminists." In this commencement address to the 2015 graduating class of Wellesley College—a women's college in Massachusetts—she outlines the unprecedented challenges and opportunities young women encounter in society today.

"That degree, and the experience of being here, is a privilege. Don't let it blind you too often."

NOTES

1 Hello class of 2015.

2 Congratulations! And thank you for that wonderful welcome. And thank you President Bottomly for that wonderful introduction.

3 I have admired Wellesley—its mission, its story, its successes—for a long time and I thank you very much for inviting me.

4 You are ridiculously lucky to be graduating from this bastion of excellence and on these beautiful acres.

5 I'm truly, truly happy to be here today, so happy, in fact, that when I found out your class color was yellow, I decided I would wear yellow eyeshadow. But on second thoughts, I realized that as much as I admire Wellesley, even yellow eyeshadow was a bit too much of a gesture. So I dug out this yellow—yellowish—headwrap instead.

6 Speaking of eyeshadow, I wasn't very interested in makeup until I was in my twenties, which is when I began to wear makeup. Because of a man. A loud, unpleasant man. He was one of the guests at a friend's dinner party. I was also a guest. I was about 23, but people often told me I looked 12. The conversation at dinner was about traditional Igbo culture, about the custom that allows only men to break the kola nut, and the kola nut[1] is a deeply symbolic part of Igbo cosmology[2].

7 I argued that it would be better if that honor were based on achievement rather than **gender**, and he looked at me and said, dismissively, "You don't know what you are talking about, you're a small girl."

8 I wanted him to disagree with the substance of my argument, but by looking at me, young and female, it was easy for him to dismiss what I said. So I decided to try to look older.

---

1. **kola nut** fruit of the kola tree, used in beverages, gum, medicine, and religious practices of West Africa
2. **cosmology** study of the universe, its foundations and physics

Please note that excerpts and passages in the StudySync® library and this workbook are intended as touchstones to generate interest in an author's work. The excerpts and passages do not substitute for the reading of entire texts, and StudySync® strongly recommends that students seek out and purchase the whole literary or informational work in order to experience it as the author intended. Links to online resellers are available in our digital library. In addition, complete works may be ordered through an authorized reseller by filling out and returning to StudySync® the order form enclosed in this workbook.

Copyright © BookheadEd Learning, LLC

9   So I thought lipstick might help. And eyeliner.

10 And I am grateful to that man because I have since come to love makeup, and its wonderful possibilities for temporary transformation.

11 So, I have not told you this anecdote as a way to illustrate my discovery of gender injustice. If anything, it's really just an ode to makeup.

12 It's really just to say that this, your graduation, is a good time to buy some lipsticks—if makeup is your sort of thing—because a good shade of lipstick can always put you in a slightly better mood on dark days.

13 It's not about my discovering gender injustice because of course I had discovered years before then. From childhood. From watching the world.

14 I already knew that the world does not extend to women the many small courtesies that it extends to men.

15 I also knew that victimhood is not a virtue. That being **discriminated** against does not make you somehow morally better.

16 And I knew that men were not inherently bad or evil. They were merely privileged[3]. And I knew that privilege blinds because it is the nature of privilege to blind.

17 I knew from this personal experience, from the class privilege I had of growing up in an educated family, that it sometimes blinded me, that I was not always as alert to the nuances of people who were different from me.

18 And you, because you now have your beautiful Wellesley degree, have become privileged, no matter what your background. That degree, and the experience of being here, is a privilege. Don't let it blind you too often. Sometimes you will need to push it aside in order to see clearly.

· · ·

19 I bring greetings to you from my mother. She's a big admirer of Wellesley, and she wishes she could be here. She called me yesterday to ask how the speech-writing was going and to tell me to remember to use a lot of lotion on my legs today so they would not look ashy.

20 My mother is 73 and she retired as the first female registrar of the University of Nigeria—which was quite a big deal at the time.

---

3. **privileged** in possession of rights or advantages not accessible to everyone

Please note that excerpts and passages in the StudySync® library and this workbook are intended as touchstones to generate interest in an author's work. The excerpts and passages do not substitute for the reading of entire texts, and StudySync® strongly recommends that students seek out and purchase the whole literary or informational work in order to experience it as the author intended. Links to online resellers are available in our digital library. In addition, complete works may be ordered through an authorized reseller by filling out and returning to StudySync® the order form enclosed in this workbook.

Copyright © BookheadEd Learning, LLC

NOTES

21 My mother likes to tell a story of the first university meeting she chaired. It was in a large conference room, and at the head of the table was a sign that said CHAIRMAN. My mother was about to get seated there when a clerk came over and made to remove the sign. All the past meetings had of course been chaired by men, and somebody had forgotten to replace the CHAIRMAN with a new sign that said CHAIRPERSON. The clerk apologized and told her he would find the new sign, since she was not a chairman.

22 My mother said no. Actually, she said, she WAS a chairman. She wanted the sign left exactly where it was. The meeting was about to begin. She didn't want anybody to think that what she was doing in that meeting at that time on that day was in any way different from what a CHAIRMAN would have done.

23 I always liked this story, and admired what I thought of as my mother's fiercely feminist choice. I once told the story to a friend, a card-carrying feminist, and I expected her to say bravo to my mother, but she was troubled by it.

24 "Why would your mother want to be called a chairman, as though she needed the MAN part to validate her?" my friend asked.

25 In some ways, I saw my friend's point.

26 Because if there were a Standard Handbook published annually by the Secret Society of Certified Feminists, then that handbook would certainly say that a woman should not be called, nor want to be called, a CHAIRMAN.

27 But gender is always about context and **circumstance**.

28 If there is a lesson in this anecdote, apart from just telling you a story about my mother to make her happy that I spoke about her at Wellesley, then it is this: Your standardized **ideologies** will not always fit your life. Because life is messy.

. . .

29 When I was growing up in Nigeria I was expected, as every student who did well was expected, to become a doctor. Deep down I knew that what I really wanted to do was to write stories. But I did what I was supposed to do and I went into medical school.

30 I told myself that I would tough it out and become a psychiatrist and that way I could use my patients' stories for my fiction.

31 But after one year of medical school I fled. I realized I would be a very unhappy doctor and I really did not want to be responsible for the inadvertent death of

Copyright © BookheadEd Learning, LLC

Please note that excerpts and passages in the StudySync® library and this workbook are intended as touchstones to generate interest in an author's work. The excerpts and passages do not substitute for the reading of entire texts, and StudySync® strongly recommends that students seek out and purchase the whole literary or informational work in order to experience it as the author intended. Links to online resellers are available in our digital library. In addition, complete works may be ordered through an authorized reseller by filling out and returning to StudySync® the order form enclosed in this workbook.

my patients. Leaving medical school was a very unusual decision, especially in Nigeria where it is very difficult to get into medical school.

32 Later, people told me that it had been very courageous of me, but I did not feel courageous at all.

33 What I felt then was not courage but a desire to make an effort. To try. I could either stay and study something that was not right for me. Or I could try and do something different. I decided to try. I took the American exams and got a scholarship to come to the US where I could study something else that was NOT related to medicine. Now it might not have worked out. I might not have been given an American scholarship.

34 My writing might not have ended up being successful. But the point is that I tried.

35 We can not always bend the world into the shapes we want but we can try, we can make a concerted and real and true effort. And you are privileged that, because of your education here, you have already been given many of the tools that you will need to try. Always just try. Because you never know.

36 And so as you graduate, as you deal with your excitement and your doubts today, I urge you to try and create the world you want to live in.

37 Minister to the world in a way that can change it. Minister radically in a real, active, practical, get your hands dirty way.

38 Wellesley will open doors for you. Walk through those doors and make your strides long and firm and sure.

39 Write television shows in which female strength is not depicted as remarkable but merely normal.

40 Teach your students to see that vulnerability is a HUMAN rather than a FEMALE trait.

41 Commission magazine articles that teach men HOW TO KEEP A WOMAN HAPPY. Because there are already too many articles that tell women how to keep a man happy. And in media interviews make sure fathers are asked how they balance family and work. In this age of 'parenting as guilt,' please spread the guilt equally. Make fathers feel as bad as mothers. Make fathers share in the glory of guilt.

42 Campaign and agitate for paid paternity leave everywhere in America.

Copyright © BookheadEd Learning, LLC

Please note that excerpts and passages in the StudySync® library and this workbook are intended as touchstones to generate interest in an author's work. The excerpts and passages do not substitute for the reading of entire texts, and StudySync® strongly recommends that students seek out and purchase the whole literary or informational work in order to experience it as the author intended. Links to online resellers are available in our digital library. In addition, complete works may be ordered through an authorized reseller by filling out and returning to StudySync® the order form enclosed in this workbook.

NOTES

43 Hire more women where there are few. But remember that a woman you hire doesn't have to be exceptionally good. Like a majority of the men who get hired, she just needs to be good enough.

. . .

44 Recently a feminist organization kindly nominated me for an important prize in a country that will remain unnamed. I was very pleased. I've been fortunate to have received a few prizes so far and I quite like them especially when they come with shiny presents. To get this prize, I was required to talk about how important a particular European feminist woman writer had been to me. Now the truth was that I had never managed to finish this feminist writer's book. It did not speak to me. It would have been a lie to claim that she had any major influence on my thinking. The truth is that I learned so much more about feminism from watching the women traders in the market in Nsukka where I grew up than from reading any **seminal** feminist text. I could have said that this woman was important to me, and I could have talked the talk, and I could have been given the prize and a shiny present.

45 But I didn't.

46 Because I had begun to ask myself what it really means to wear this FEMINIST label so publicly.

47 Just as I asked myself after excerpts of my feminism speech were used in a song by a talented musician whom I think some of you might know. I thought it was a very good thing that the word 'feminist' would be introduced to a new generation.

48 But I was startled by how many people, many of whom were academics, saw something troubling, even menacing, in this.

49 It was as though feminism was supposed to be an elite little cult, with esoteric rites of membership.

50 But it shouldn't. Feminism should be an inclusive party. Feminism should be a party full of different feminisms.

51 And so, class of 2015, please go out there and make Feminism a big raucous inclusive party.

. . .

52 The past three weeks have been the most emotionally difficult of my life. My father is 83 years old, a retired professor of statistics, a lovely kind man. I am an absolute Daddy's girl. Three weeks ago, he was kidnapped near his home

Please note that excerpts and passages in the StudySync® library and this workbook are intended as touchstones to generate interest in an author's work. The excerpts and passages do not substitute for the reading of entire texts, and StudySync® strongly recommends that students seek out and purchase the whole literary or informational work in order to experience it as the author intended. Links to online resellers are available in our digital library. In addition, complete works may be ordered through an authorized reseller by filling out and returning to StudySync® the order form enclosed in this workbook.

Copyright © BookheadEd Learning, LLC

NOTES

in Nigeria. And for a number of days, my family and I went through the kind of emotional pain that I have never known in my life. We were talking to threatening strangers on the phone, begging and negotiating for my father's safety and we were not always sure if my father was alive. He was released after we paid a ransom. He is well, in fairly good shape and in his usual lovely way, is very keen to reassure us all that he is fine.

53 I am still not sleeping well, I still wake up many times at night, in panic, worried that something else has gone wrong, I still cannot look at my father without fighting tears, without feeling this profound relief and gratitude that he is safe, but also rage that he had to undergo such an indignity to his body and to his spirit.

54 And the experience has made me rethink many things, what truly matters, and what doesn't. What I value, and what I don't.

55 And as you graduate today, I urge you to think about that a little more. Think about what really matters to you. Think about what you WANT to really matter to you.

56 I read about your rather lovely tradition of referring to older students as "big sisters" and younger ones as "little sisters." And I read about the rather strange thing about being thrown into the pond—and I didn't really get that—but I would very much like to be your honorary big sister today.

57 Which means that I would like to give you bits of advice as your big sister:

58 All over the world, girls are raised to be make themselves likeable, to twist themselves into shapes that suit other people.

59 Please do not twist yourself into shapes to please. Don't do it. If someone likes that version of you, that version of you that is false and holds back, then they actually just like that twisted shape, and not you. And the world is such a gloriously multifaceted, diverse place that there are people in the world who will like you, the real you, as you are.

60 I am lucky that my writing has given me a platform that I choose to use to talk about things that I care about, and I have said a few things that have not been so popular with a number of people. I have been told to shut up about certain things – such as my position on the equal rights of gay people on the continent of Africa, such as my deeply held belief that men and women are completely equal. I don't speak to provoke. I speak because I think our time on earth is short and each moment that we are not our truest selves, each moment we pretend to be what we are not, each moment we say what we do not mean because we imagine that is what somebody wants us to say, then we are wasting our time on earth.

Copyright © BookheadEd Learning, LLC

Please note that excerpts and passages in the StudySync® library and this workbook are intended as touchstones to generate interest in an author's work. The excerpts and passages do not substitute for the reading of entire texts, and StudySync® strongly recommends that students seek out and purchase the whole literary or informational work in order to experience it as the author intended. Links to online resellers are available in our digital library. In addition, complete works may be ordered through an authorized reseller by filling out and returning to StudySync® the order form enclosed in this workbook.

NOTES

61   I don't mean to sound precious but please don't waste your time on earth, but there is one exception. The only acceptable way of wasting your time on earth is online shopping.

62   Okay, one last thing about my mother. My mother and I do not agree on many things regarding gender. There are certain things my mother believes a person should do, for the simple reason that said person 'is a woman.' Such as nod occasionally and smile even when smiling is the last thing one wants to do. Such as strategically give in to certain arguments, especially when arguing with a non-female. Such as get married and have children. I can think of fairly good reasons for doing any of these. But 'because you are a woman' is not one of them. And so, Class of 2015, never ever accept 'Because You Are A Woman' as a reason for doing or not doing anything.

63   And, finally I would like to end with a final note on the most important thing in the world: love.

64   Now girls are often raised to see love only as giving. Women are praised for their love when that love is an act of giving. But to love is to give AND to take.

65   Please love by giving and by taking. Give and be given. If you are only giving and not taking, you'll know. You'll know from that small and true voice inside you that we females are so often socialized to silence.

66   Don't silence that voice. Dare to take.

67   Congratulations.

Copyright @ 2015 by Chimamanda Ngozi Adichie, used by permission of The Wylie Agency LLC.

Copyright © BookheadEd Learning, LLC

Please note that excerpts and passages in the StudySync® library and this workbook are intended as touchstones to generate interest in an author's work. The excerpts and passages do not substitute for the reading of entire texts, and StudySync® strongly recommends that students seek out and purchase the whole literary or informational work in order to experience it as the author intended. Links to online resellers are available in our digital library. In addition, complete works may be ordered through an authorized reseller by filling out and returning to StudySync® the order form enclosed in this workbook.

WRITE

PERSONAL RESPONSE: In her speech, Chimamanda Ngozi Adichie uses personal memories and stories to explain how small gestures of resistance (wearing makeup, or wanting to be called a "chairman" instead of "chairperson," for example) have helped her and her mother be true to themselves, notwithstanding other people's attempts to transform them into something they are not. Think about your own identity. Has anyone ever pushed you to be something other than your true self? Write a brief speech that describes this situation and the outcome. Were you able to remain true to yourself, or did you have to compromise? Why is it important to be true to yourself? Why is it important for others to acknowledge your true self? (If you have never experienced such a situation, please imagine one and write your speech based on that.)

Copyright © BookheadEd Learning, LLC

Please note that excerpts and passages in the StudySync® library and this workbook are intended as touchstones to generate interest in an author's work. The excerpts and passages do not substitute for the reading of entire texts, and StudySync® strongly recommends that students seek out and purchase the whole literary or informational work in order to experience it as the author intended. Links to online resellers are available in our digital library. In addition, complete works may be ordered through an authorized reseller by filling out and returning to StudySync® the order form enclosed in this workbook.

Reading & Writing Companion   95

Plessy v. Ferguson

INFORMATIONAL TEXT
U.S. Supreme Court
1896

Introduction

Plessy v. Ferguson was an 1896 U.S. Supreme Court case that allowed segregation of public facilities under the doctrine of "separate but equal." The underlying case was orchestrated by a committee of concerned citizens who opposed a Louisiana law that required separate railroad cars for blacks and whites. Plaintiff Homer Plessy, a man with one-eighth African blood, challenged that law when he attempted to ride as a passenger on a whites-only car on the East Louisiana Railroad and refused requests to leave. He was found guilty by Judge John Howard Ferguson, who ruled that Louisiana had the right to regulate railroad companies that operated within the state. The Supreme Court's ruling that "separate but equal" was not in violation of the constitution was eventually invalidated by

"The judgment of the court below is therefore affirmed."

From the majority opinion of the Court, delivered by Justice Henry Billings Brown:

NOTES

1 The constitutionality[1] of this act is attacked upon the ground that it conflicts both with the thirteenth amendment of the constitution, abolishing slavery, and the fourteenth amendment[2], which prohibits certain restrictive legislation on the part of the states.

A man drinks from a streetcar station water fountain labeled "COLORED" in 1939, over forty years after the Plessy v. Ferguson decision.

2 1. That it does not conflict with the thirteenth amendment, which abolished slavery and involuntary servitude, except as a punishment for crime, is too clear for argument. Slavery implies involuntary servitude,—a state of bondage; the ownership of mankind as a chattel, or, at least, the control of the labor and services of one man for the benefit of another, and the absence of a legal right to the disposal of his own person, property, and services. This amendment was said in the Slaughter-House Cases to have been intended primarily to abolish slavery, as it had been previously known in this country and that it equally forbade Mexican peonage or the Chinese coolie trade, when they amounted to slavery or involuntary servitude, and that the use of the word "servitude" was intended to prohibit the use of all forms of involuntary slavery, of whatever class or name. It was **intimated,** however, in that case, that this amendment was regarded by the statesmen of that day as insufficient to protect the colored race from certain laws which had been enacted in the Southern states, imposing upon the colored race **onerous** disabilities and burdens, and curtailing their rights in the pursuit of life, liberty, and property to such an

> **Skill:**
> Reasons and Evidence
>
> *Justice Brown argues that the act (by plaintiff Homer Plessy) is unconstitutional. He supports his opinion by referring to two constitutional amendments. His position seems clear and based on constitutional reasoning.*

---

1. **constitutionality** the extent to which something adheres to the rules and principles laid forth in a Constitution
2. **amendment** an addition or addendum to the U.S. Constitution (there have been 27 to date)

Please note that excerpts and passages in the StudySync® library and this workbook are intended as touchstones to generate interest in an author's work. The excerpts and passages do not substitute for the reading of entire texts, and StudySync® strongly recommends that students seek out and purchase the whole literary or informational work in order to experience it as the author intended. Links to online resellers are available in our digital library. In addition, complete works may be ordered through an authorized reseller by filling out and returning to StudySync® the order form enclosed in this workbook.

Copyright © BookheadEd Learning, LLC

NOTES

extent that their freedom was of little value; and that the fourteenth amendment was devised to meet this **exigency.**

. . .

3   2. By the fourteenth amendment, all persons born or naturalized in the United States, and subject to the jurisdiction[3] thereof, are made citizens of the United States and of the state wherein they reside; and the states are forbidden from making or enforcing any law which shall **abridge** the privileges or immunities of citizens of the United States, or shall deprive any person of life, liberty, or property without due process of law, or deny to any person within their jurisdiction the equal protection of the laws.

. . .

4   The object of the amendment was undoubtedly to enforce the absolute equality of the two races before the law, but, in the nature of things, it could not have been intended to abolish distinctions based upon color, or to enforce social, as distinguished from political, equality, or a commingling of the two races upon terms unsatisfactory to either. Laws permitting, and even requiring, their separation, in places where they are liable to be brought into contact, do not necessarily imply the inferiority of either race to the other, and have been generally, if not universally, recognized as within the competency of the state legislatures in the exercise of their police power. The most common instance of this is connected with the establishment of separate schools for white and colored children, which have been held to be a valid exercise of the legislative power even by courts of states where the political rights of the colored race have been longest and most earnestly enforced.

. . .

**Skill:
Rhetoric**

Brown's argument continues in a logical progression. He says that equality cannot be achieved by legally-enforced commingling. Can equality be achieved by legally-enforced separation? There is a breakdown in logic and rhetoric.

5   We consider the underlying **fallacy** of the plaintiff's argument to consist in the assumption that the enforced separation of the two races stamps the colored race with a badge of inferiority. If this be so, it is not by reason of anything found in the act, but solely because the colored race chooses to put that construction upon it. The argument necessarily assumes that if, as has been more than once the case, and is not unlikely to be so again, the colored race should become the dominant power in the state legislature, and should enact a law in precisely similar terms, it would thereby **relegate** the white race to an inferior position. We imagine that the white race, at least, would not acquiesce in this assumption. The argument also assumes that social prejudices may be overcome by legislation, and that equal rights cannot be secured to the negro except by an enforced commingling of the two races. We cannot

---

3. **jurisdiction** an area in which a government has power or a set of laws is used

Please note that excerpts and passages in the StudySync® library and this workbook are intended as touchstones to generate interest in an author's work. The excerpts and passages do not substitute for the reading of entire texts, and StudySync® strongly recommends that students seek out and purchase the whole literary or informational work in order to experience it as the author intended. Links to online resellers are available in our digital library. In addition, complete works may be ordered through an authorized reseller by filling out and returning to StudySync® the order form enclosed in this workbook.

Copyright © BookheadEd Learning, LLC

NOTES

accept this proposition. If the two races are to meet upon terms of social equality, it must be the result of natural affinities, a mutual appreciation of each other's merits, and a voluntary consent of individuals. As was said by the court of appeals of New York in People v. Gallagher: 'This end can neither be accomplished nor promoted by laws which conflict with the general sentiment of the community upon whom they are designed to operate. When the government, therefore, has secured to each of its citizens equal rights before the law, and equal opportunities for improvement and progress, it has accomplished the end for which it was organized, and performed all of the functions respecting social advantages with which it is endowed.' Legislation is powerless to **eradicate** racial instincts, or to abolish distinctions based upon physical differences, and the attempt to do so can only result in accentuating the difficulties of the present situation. If the civil and political rights of both races be equal, one cannot be inferior to the other civilly or politically. If one race be inferior to the other socially, the constitution of the United States cannot put them upon the same plane.

6   It is true that the question of the proportion of colored blood necessary to constitute a colored person, as distinguished from a white person, is one upon which there is a difference of opinion in the different states; some holding that any visible admixture of black blood stamps the person as belonging to the colored race; others, that it depends upon the preponderance of blood; and still others, that the predominance of white blood must only be in the proportion of three-fourths. But these are questions to be determined under the laws of each state, and are not properly put in issue in this case. Under the allegations of his petition, it may undoubtedly become a question of importance whether, under the laws of Louisiana, the petitioner belongs to the white or colored race.

7   The judgment of the court below is therefore affirmed.

From Justice John Marshall Harlan's dissenting opinion:

8   The thirteenth amendment does not permit the withholding or the deprivation of any right necessarily inhering in freedom. It not only struck down the institution of slavery as previously existing in the United States, but it prevents the imposition of any burdens or disabilities that constitute badges of slavery or servitude. It decreed universal civil freedom in this country. This court has so adjudged. But, that amendment having been found inadequate to the protection of the rights of those who had been in slavery, it was followed by the fourteenth amendment, which added greatly to the dignity and glory of American citizenship, and to the security of personal liberty, by declaring that 'all persons born or naturalized in the United States, and subject to the jurisdiction thereof, are citizens of the United States and of the state wherein they reside,' and that 'no state shall make or enforce any law which shall

Skill:
Technical
Language

The use of the word *right* is crucial to Harlan's argument. This is a Supreme Court opinion so it has major consequences for civil rights in America. He uses the Thirteenth Amendment to argue for all rights associated with freedom.

Copyright © BookheadEd Learning, LLC

Please note that excerpts and passages in the StudySync® library and this workbook are intended as touchstones to generate interest in an author's work. The excerpts and passages do not substitute for the reading of entire texts, and StudySync® strongly recommends that students seek out and purchase the whole literary or informational work in order to experience it as the author intended. Links to online resellers are available in our digital library. In addition, complete works may be ordered through an authorized reseller by filling out and returning to StudySync® the order form enclosed in this workbook.

NOTES

abridge the privileges or immunities of citizens of the United States; nor shall any state deprive any person of life, liberty or property without due process of law, nor deny to any person within its jurisdiction the equal protection of the laws.' These two amendments, if enforced according to their true intent and meaning, will protect all the civil rights that pertain to freedom and citizenship. Finally, and to the end that no citizen should be denied, on account of his race, the privilege of participating in the political control of his country, it was declared by the fifteenth amendment that 'the right of citizens of the United States to vote shall not be denied or abridged by the United States or by any state on account of race, color or previous condition of servitude.'

9   These notable additions to the fundamental law were welcomed by the friends of liberty throughout the world. They removed the race line from our governmental systems. They had, as this court has said, a common purpose, namely, to secure 'to a race recently emancipated, a race that through many generations have been held in slavery, all the civil rights that the superior race enjoy.' They declared, in legal effect, this court has further said, 'that the law in the states shall be the same for the black as for the white; that all persons, whether colored or white, shall stand equal before the laws of the states; and in regard to the colored race, for whose protection the amendment was primarily designed, that no discrimination shall be made against them by law because of their color.' We also said: 'The words of the amendment, it is true, are prohibitory, but they contain a necessary implication of a positive immunity or right, most valuable to the colored race,—the right to exemption from unfriendly legislation against them distinctively as colored; exemption from legal discriminations, implying inferiority in civil society, lessening the security of their enjoyment of the rights which others enjoy; and discriminations which are steps towards reducing them to the condition of a subject race.' It was, consequently, adjudged that a state law that excluded citizens of the colored race from juries, because of their race, however well qualified in other respects to discharge the duties of jurymen, was repugnant to the fourteenth amendment. At the present term, referring to the previous adjudications, this court declared that 'underlying all of those decisions is the principle that the constitution of the United States, in its present form, forbids, so far as civil and political rights are concerned, discrimination by the general government or the states against any citizen because of his race. All citizens are equal before the law.'

10   The decisions referred to show the scope of the recent amendments of the constitution. They also show that it is not within the power of a state to prohibit colored citizens, because of their race, from participating as jurors in the administration of justice.

Copyright © BookheadEd Learning, LLC

Please note that excerpts and passages in the StudySync® library and this workbook are intended as touchstones to generate interest in an author's work. The excerpts and passages do not substitute for the reading of entire texts, and StudySync® strongly recommends that students seek out and purchase the whole literary or informational work in order to experience it as the author intended. Links to online resellers are available in our digital library. In addition, complete works may be ordered through an authorized reseller by filling out and returning to StudySync® the order form enclosed in this workbook.

11 It was said in argument that the statute of Louisiana does not discriminate against either race, but prescribes a rule applicable alike to white and colored citizens. But this argument does not meet the difficulty. Every one knows that the statute in question had its origin in the purpose, not so much to exclude white persons from railroad cars occupied by blacks, as to exclude colored people from coaches occupied by or assigned to white persons. Railroad corporations of Louisiana did not make discrimination among whites in the matter of commodation for travelers. The thing to accomplish was, under the guise of giving equal accommodation for whites and blacks, to compel the latter to keep to themselves while traveling in railroad passenger coaches. No one would be so wanting in candor as to assert the contrary. The fundamental objection, therefore, to the statute, is that it interferes with the personal freedom of citizens. 'Personal liberty,' it has been well said, 'consists in the power of locomotion, of changing situation, or removing one's person to whatsoever places one's own inclination may direct, without imprisonment or restraint, unless by due course of law.' If a white man and a black man choose to occupy the same public conveyance on a public highway, it is their right to do so; and no government, proceeding alone on grounds of race, can prevent it without infringing the personal liberty of each.

· · ·

12 The sure guaranty of the peace and security of each race is the clear, distinct, unconditional recognition by our governments, national and state, of every right that inheres in civil freedom, and of the equality before the law of all citizens of the United States, without regard to race. State enactments regulating the enjoyment of civil rights upon the basis of race, and cunningly devised to defeat legitimate results of the war, under the pretense of recognizing equality of rights, can have no other result than to render permanent peace impossible, and to keep alive a conflict of races, the continuance of which must do harm to all concerned.

Skill:
Technical
Language

Harlan uses right *again, this time with a specific example. He associates the term with personal liberty and with freedom. He states that legislating the separation of races infringes on the liberty and freedom of all races.*

Copyright © BookheadEd Learning, LLC

Please note that excerpts and passages in the StudySync® library and this workbook are intended as touchstones to generate interest in an author's work. The excerpts and passages do not substitute for the reading of entire texts, and StudySync® strongly recommends that students seek out and purchase the whole literary or informational work in order to experience it as the author intended. Links to online resellers are available in our digital library. In addition, complete works may be ordered through an authorized reseller by filling out and returning to StudySync® the order form enclosed in this workbook.

Reading & Writing Companion   **101**

First Read

Read *Plessy v. Ferguson.* After you read, complete the Think Questions below.

THINK QUESTIONS

1. Refer to one or more details from the text to explain what Justice Brown believes to be the limitations of the Supreme Court's power. What words and phrases hint at why he feels the Court has this limit?

2. According to Justice Brown, who is at fault if one group of people feels inferior to another? How do you think he would suggest Plessy deal with the segregation laws? Support your answer with textual evidence.

3. According to Justice Harlan, what did the railroad claim was its motivation for the decision to separate passengers? How does Harlan feel about that claim, and what does he think the real motivation was? Use details from the text to describe Justice Harlan's response to the railroad's actions and the arguments made in court.

4. Use sentence clues, such as contextual definitions or restatements, to determine the meaning of the word **relegate**. Verify that your determined meaning makes sense by checking it in the context of the sentence or paragraph. Write your definition here and explain how you determined and verified it.

5. Use contextual clues to determine the meaning of the word **eradicate**. Write your definition here and tell how you found it. Then, consult a reference work, such as a dictionary, to check your definition and trace the etymology of "eradicate." Explain how knowing the word's Latin roots helps you to understand its full meaning.

Copyright © BookheadEd Learning, LLC

Please note that excerpts and passages in the StudySync® library and this workbook are intended as touchstones to generate interest in an author's work. The excerpts and passages do not substitute for the reading of entire texts, and StudySync® strongly recommends that students seek out and purchase the whole literary or informational work in order to experience it as the author intended. Links to online resellers are available in our digital library. In addition, complete works may be ordered through an authorized reseller by filling out and returning to StudySync® the order form enclosed in this workbook.

Skill:
Reasons and Evidence

Use the Checklist to analyze Reasons and Evidence in *Plessy v. Ferguson*. Refer to the sample student annotations about Reasons and Evidence in the text.

••• CHECKLIST FOR REASONS AND EVIDENCE

In order to delineate and evaluate the reasoning in seminal (influential) U.S. texts, note the following:

✓ the writer's position and determine how he or she uses legal reasoning to interpret the law

  • legal reasoning includes the thinking processes and strategies used by lawyers and judges when arguing and deciding legal cases, and is based on constitutional principles, or laws written down in the U.S. Constitution

✓ a Supreme Court judge that disagrees with the legal reasoning behind the majority opinion in a legal case writes a dissent, expressing opposition

  • a dissent must follow constitutional principles, or the laws set down in the Constitution

✓ determine whether the premise is based on legal reasoning and constitutional principles

To evaluate the reasoning in seminal (influential) U.S. texts, including the application of constitutional principles and use of legal reasoning, consider the following questions:

✓ What position does the writer take?

✓ How does the writer use constitutional principles and legal reasoning to support his or her position?

Copyright © BookheadEd Learning, LLC

Please note that excerpts and passages in the StudySync® library and this workbook are intended as touchstones to generate interest in an author's work. The excerpts and passages do not substitute for the reading of entire texts, and StudySync® strongly recommends that students seek out and purchase the whole literary or informational work in order to experience it as the author intended. Links to online resellers are available in our digital library. In addition, complete works may be ordered through an authorized reseller by filling out and returning to StudySync® the order form enclosed in this workbook.

Reading & Writing Companion   **103**

Skill:
Reasons and Evidence

Reread paragraph 5 of *Plessy v. Ferguson*. Then, using the Checklist on the previous page, answer the multiple-choice questions below.

 YOUR TURN

1. This question has two parts. First, answer Part A. Then, answer Part B.

   Part A: Why does Justice Brown quote the previous Supreme Court decision *People v. Gallagher* during this part of his argument?

   ○ A. He uses a previous Supreme Court decision to support his argument that courts can only enforce political and not social equality.

   ○ B. He uses a previous Supreme Court decision to support his argument that the racial discrimination in public places should be outlawed.

   ○ C. He uses a previous Supreme Court decision to refute the Louisiana state law.

   ○ D. He uses a previous Supreme Court decision to support his argument that the U.S. Constitution should make distinctions based on race.

   Part B: Which of the following statements best represents Justice Brown's reasoning in relation to the answer in Part A?

   ○ A. "If the two races are to meet upon terms of social equality, it must be the result of natural affinities, a mutual appreciation of each other's merits, and a voluntary consent of individuals."

   ○ B. "If one race be inferior to the other socially, the constitution of the United States cannot put them upon the same plane."

   ○ C. "If the civil and political rights of both races be equal, one cannot be inferior to the other civilly or politically."

   ○ D. "Legislation is powerless to eradicate racial instincts, or to abolish distinctions based upon physical differences, and the attempt to do so can only result in accentuating the difficulties of the present situation."

Copyright © BookheadEd Learning, LLC

Please note that excerpts and passages in the StudySync® library and this workbook are intended as touchstones to generate interest in an author's work. The excerpts and passages do not substitute for the reading of entire texts, and StudySync® strongly recommends that students seek out and purchase the whole literary or informational work in order to experience it as the author intended. Links to online resellers are available in our digital library. In addition, complete works may be ordered through an authorized reseller by filling out and returning to StudySync® the order form enclosed in this workbook.

Skill: Rhetoric

Use the Checklist to analyze Rhetoric in *Plessy v. Ferguson*. Refer to the sample student annotations about Rhetoric in the text.

••• CHECKLIST FOR RHETORIC

In order to identify an author's point of view or purpose in a text, note the following:

✓ the purpose of the text

✓ the way in which a writer phrases, or constructs, what he or she wants to say

✓ details and statements that identify the author's point of view or purposes

To identify how the author uses rhetorical appeals, look for:

✓ the three elements of persuasion as defined by Aristotle: ethos, pathos, and logos. Ethos relies on the authority or credibility of the person making the argument to try to convince an audience. Pathos is an appeal to emotion. Logos is an appeal to reason or logic

✓ a specific style, such as the use of assonance or the repetition of certain words can be used to create catchphrases, something that can be widely or repeatedly used and is easily remembered

✓ when the author's use of rhetorical appeal is particularly effective

To determine the rhetorical appeal(s) in a text in which the rhetoric is particularly effective, consider the following questions:

✓ Which rhetorical appeals can you identify in the text?

✓ How does this writer or speaker use rhetorical devices or appeals to persuade an audience?

✓ In what way are the rhetorical devices particularly effective?

Copyright © BookheadEd Learning, LLC

Please note that excerpts and passages in the StudySync® library and this workbook are intended as touchstones to generate interest in an author's work. The excerpts and passages do not substitute for the reading of entire texts, and StudySync® strongly recommends that students seek out and purchase the whole literary or informational work in order to experience it as the author intended. Links to online resellers are available in our digital library. In addition, complete works may be ordered through an authorized reseller by filling out and returning to StudySync® the order form enclosed in this workbook.

Reading & Writing Companion **105**

Skill: Rhetoric

Reread paragraph 9 of *Plessy v. Ferguson*. Then, using the Checklist on the previous page, answer the multiple-choice questions below.

⟳ YOUR TURN

1. Which of the following states the main rhetorical strategy of the passage?

   ○ A. An appeal to emotions causing a sense of disgust
   ○ B. An appeal to shared beliefs based on the concept of freedom
   ○ C. An appeal to morals causing a sense of guilt
   ○ D. An appeal to the intellect based on data and statistics

2. Which sentence or phrase from the passage best supports your answer to Question 1?

   ○ A. These notable additions to the fundamental law were welcomed by the friends of liberty throughout the world.
   ○ B. They declared, in legal effect, this court has further said, "that the law in the states shall be the same for the black as for the white."
   ○ C. "That all persons, whether colored or white, shall stand equal before the laws of the states."
   ○ D. All of the above

Copyright © BookheadEd Learning, LLC

Please note that excerpts and passages in the StudySync® library and this workbook are intended as touchstones to generate interest in an author's work. The excerpts and passages do not substitute for the reading of entire texts, and StudySync® strongly recommends that students seek out and purchase the whole literary or informational work in order to experience it as the author intended. Links to online resellers are available in our digital library. In addition, complete works may be ordered through an authorized reseller by filling out and returning to StudySync® the order form enclosed in this workbook.

Skill:
Technical Language

Use the Checklist to analyze Technical Language in *Plessy v. Ferguson*. Refer to the sample student annotations about Technical Language in the text.

••• CHECKLIST FOR TECHNICAL LANGUAGE

In order to determine the meaning of words and phrases as they are used in a text, including key terms and technical meanings, note the following:

✓ the subject of the book or article

✓ any unfamiliar words that you think might be technical terms

✓ words that have multiple meanings that change when used with a specific subject

✓ the possible contextual meaning of a word, or the definition from a dictionary

✓ key terms that are used repeatedly throughout the text

To determine the meaning of words and phrases as they are used in a text, including key terms and technical meanings, consider the following questions:

✓ What is the subject of the informational text?

✓ How does the use of technical language help establish the author as an authority on the subject?

✓ Are there any key terms or technical words that have an impact on the meaning and tone of the book or article?

✓ Does the author use the same term several times, refining its meaning and adding layers to it over the course of the text?

Copyright © BookheadEd Learning, LLC

Please note that excerpts and passages in the StudySync® library and this workbook are intended as touchstones to generate interest in an author's work. The excerpts and passages do not substitute for the reading of entire texts, and StudySync® strongly recommends that students seek out and purchase the whole literary or informational work in order to experience it as the author intended. Links to online resellers are available in our digital library. In addition, complete works may be ordered through an authorized reseller by filling out and returning to StudySync® the order form enclosed in this workbook.

Reading & Writing Companion   **107**

Skill: Technical Language

Reread paragraph 2 of *Plessy v. Ferguson*. Then, using the Checklist on the previous page, answer the multiple-choice questions below.

⟳ YOUR TURN

1. What is the most likely reason why Justice Brown defines the term *slavery* in his argument?

   ○ A. Justice Brown defines the term *slavery* because he believes the opposing argument wants to make slavery legal again in America.

   ○ B. Justice Brown defines the term *slavery* because making a technical term of slavery allows Justice Brown to argue that the Thirteenth amendment is not being violated.

   ○ C. Justice Brown defines the term *slavery* because he wants the court to understand how the separation of the races is similar to slavery.

   ○ D. Justice Brown defines the term *slavery* because making a technical term of slavery allows him to argue that the Thirteenth amendment is being violated.

2. What does Justice Brown state is the function of the technical term *involuntary servitude* in the Thirteenth Amendment?

   ○ A. *Involuntary servitude* provides a more specific definition of the concept of slavery so that the Thirteenth Amendment only protects some individuals.

   ○ B. *Involuntary servitude* refutes the claim that slavery was involuntary servitude, so the Thirteenth Amendment should be abolished.

   ○ C. *Involuntary servitude* generalizes the concept of slavery to protect the freedom of any person, whether they are legally designated as "slaves" or not.

   ○ D. *Involuntary servitude* has multiple contextual meanings, so it is important to understand what it means in the context of the Thirteenth Amendment.

Copyright © BookheadEd Learning, LLC

Please note that excerpts and passages in the StudySync® library and this workbook are intended as touchstones to generate interest in an author's work. The excerpts and passages do not substitute for the reading of entire texts, and StudySync® strongly recommends that students seek out and purchase the whole literary or informational work in order to experience it as the author intended. Links to online resellers are available in our digital library. In addition, complete works may be ordered through an authorized reseller by filling out and returning to StudySync® the order form enclosed in this workbook.

Close Read

Reread *Plessy v. Ferguson*. As you reread, complete the Skills Focus questions below. Then use your answers and annotations from the questions to help you complete the Write activity.

◎ SKILLS FOCUS

1. Explain why Justice Harlan, in the first two paragraphs of the dissenting opinion, also mentions the Fifteenth Amendment. How does this relate to the case of *Plessy v. Ferguson*? Use the annotation tool to highlight details from the text that helped you form your explanation.

2. How do Justices Brown and Harlan use the Thirteenth Amendment to provide reasons and evidence for their arguments? Do they agree or disagree with each other on how the Thirteenth Amendment relates to the case at hand? Highlight textual evidence that expresses their interpretations and their similarities or differences.

3. Reread the last paragraph of the reading selection. Summarize Justice Harlan's argument here and explain what kind of rhetorical strategy he uses to discredit the Louisiana railroad's statute and the

claims of Justice Brown's majority opinion. Highlight textual evidence that supports your explanation.

4. Throughout their arguments, Justice Brown and Justice Harlan both refer extensively to several amendments. What is the effect of using the technical term "amendment" on their speech and reasoning? Do both justices use the term in the same way? Highlight textual evidence to support your answer.

5. Reread the last two paragraphs of Justice Harlan's argument. In what way might Harlan's position reflect changing attitudes toward American citizenship and American values? How does Harlan's understanding of race and equal rights suggest the potential for a different kind of future in America? Highlight textual evidence to support your answer.

✏ WRITE

COMPARE AND CONTRAST: Compare and contrast the arguments in Justice Brown's majority opinion with Justice Harlan's dissenting opinion in *Plessy v. Ferguson*. Which rhetorical strategies does each use most effectively to advance their arguments? Which arguments or instances of legal reasoning don't seem to have withstood the test of time? Explain your response using textual evidence from each argument.

Copyright © BookheadEd Learning, LLC

Please note that excerpts and passages in the StudySync® library and this workbook are intended as touchstones to generate interest in an author's work. The excerpts and passages do not substitute for the reading of entire texts, and StudySync® strongly recommends that students seek out and purchase the whole literary or informational work in order to experience it as the author intended. Links to online resellers are available in our digital library. In addition, complete works may be ordered through an authorized reseller by filling out and returning to StudySync® the order form enclosed in this workbook.

Reading & Writing Companion   **109**

Booster Staff Investigates

INFORMATIONAL TEXT
Maddie Baden, Connor Balthazor,
Gina Mathew, Trina Paul,
Kali Poenitske, & Patrick Sullivan
2017

Introduction

Juniors and seniors from Pittsburg High School in Pittsburg, Kansas made headlines, and history, in March of 2017. Six members of the high school newspaper—Maddie Baden, Connor Balthazor, Gina Mathew, Trina Paul, Kali Poenitske and Patrick Sullivan—uncovered the fraudulent past of their newly inducted principal with a lot of determination and a little help from Google. These members of *The Booster Redux* staff contributed to this article, which not only shed light on the discrepancies of the new administrator's educational credentials but also took down a "university" that wasn't what it seemed. The students' hard-hitting journalism caught the attention of news outlets around the world, proving that determined young people can make a difference.

"*The Booster* staff found inconsistencies in Robertson's credentials."

NOTES

1 Following the hiring of incoming Pittsburg High School (PHS) principal Dr. Amy Robertson on March 6, discrepancies arose between Robertson's personal accounts of her education and information provided by education institutions she said she attended. The discrepancies cast doubt on the **accreditation** of a university she said she attended and the degrees she listed. Robertson said she currently works as the CEO of an education consulting firm known as Atticus I S Consultants in Dubai, and has resided there for over 20 years. According to a Pittsburg Community Schools press release on Thursday, Robertson "gained leadership and management experience at the international equivalence of a building administrator and superintendent. As CEO, she advised global companies on education projects, including writing and implementing curriculum and school policies, developing and executing professional development, and advising on school construction and renovation projects."

2 Robertson said she will arrive in the US in April and is eager for the new experience. "I'm excited about the opportunity," Robertson said. "I could easily stay [in Dubai] for another 10 years working in schools as a principal here, but I want to come home. I want to be in the US, and I want to be a part of a community. Pittsburg is the right community to put down roots in." *The Booster Redux* staff typically introduces each new administrator at PHS with a news story. During the interview process with Robertson, *The Booster* staff found **inconsistencies** in Robertson's credentials. The staff presented these concerns to Pittsburg Community School superintendent Destry Brown, who encouraged *The Booster* reporters to reach out to Robertson. On March 16, *The Booster* staff held a conference call with the incoming principal. *Booster* adviser Emily Smith and Brown were also present. During the call, Robertson presented incomplete answers, conflicting dates and inconsistencies in her responses.

3 After the conference call interview, the staff conducted further research online and by phone interview to confirm her credentials. These are the findings.

Copyright © BookheadEd Learning, LLC

Please note that excerpts and passages in the StudySync® library and this workbook are intended as touchstones to generate interest in an author's work. The excerpts and passages do not substitute for the reading of entire texts, and StudySync® strongly recommends that students seek out and purchase the whole literary or informational work in order to experience it as the author intended. Links to online resellers are available in our digital library. In addition, complete works may be ordered through an authorized reseller by filling out and returning to StudySync® the order form enclosed in this workbook.

Educational Background

4   Robertson said in the conference call interview she earned a Master's degree in Comparative Literature and a Ph.D. in English from Corllins University. Corllins, however, has been under fire in the national media for its lack of **legitimacy**. Furthermore, the Better Business Bureau's website said, "This business is not BBB accredited." The posting online in 2010 also stated, "The true physical address of Corllins University is unknown." Robertson said during the conference call interview that the majority of her education through this university was done online, but that she also occasionally traveled to the onsite campus in Stockton, Calif. "In 1994, I was living in Spain," Robertson said during the conference call interview. "I kept my apartment in New York at the time. I would fly back and forth [from Spain] to New York and California all the time."

5   When asked by Brown if she took classes in Stockton, Calif. during two different summers, Robertson replied that she had. However, a check of the records at the City of Stockton's Community Development Department **indicated** that no business license or building permit existed for Corllins University, as stated by City of Stockton permit technician Carmen Davila.

6   "If they're going to do business, then they need to have a business license," Davila said via phone interview. "I don't have any business license under that name. I don't think we have a [Corllins University] here in the area."

7   Stockton is located in San Joaquin County. The San Joaquin Community Development Department records also indicated that no such university ever existed in Stockton.

8   "In our business records, we have no such record of Corllins University existing," Megan Aguirre, an associate planner of the department in San Joaquin County, said via phone interview with *The Booster*. Corllins is not accredited by the U.S. Department of Education. Accreditation is a status given to colleges and universities deemed **valid** educational institutions. The department's online database of both accredited online and traditional colleges and universities returned no past or current record of Corllins. When asked if a degree from Corllins University would be accepted, Pittsburg State University Registrar Debbie Greve could not find any record of the existence of Corllins. "[Corllins] is not in the book at all, so I would doubt the accreditation of that school," Greve said. "[If they had ever been accredited], they would be listed in this book. Because if they had ever been accredited, it lists them as accredited and it shows the period of time in which they were accredited. It sounds like they're trying to pass themselves off as accredited but, in fact, they maybe fell short of that."

9   Further research seems to show Corllins University is considered a diploma mill, or a "business that sells fake college degrees," according to Oregon

Copyright © BookheadEd Learning, LLC

Please note that excerpts and passages in the StudySync® library and this workbook are intended as touchstones to generate interest in an author's work. The excerpts and passages do not substitute for the reading of entire texts, and StudySync® strongly recommends that students seek out and purchase the whole literary or informational work in order to experience it as the author intended. Links to online resellers are available in our digital library. In addition, complete works may be ordered through an authorized reseller by filling out and returning to StudySync® the order form enclosed in this workbook.

Live, the website of *The Oregonian*. The university is listed as one of the "top 10 sources of invalid degree reports or **inquiries**" received by the Oregon Office of Degree Authorization. According to its website, Corllins University has two accreditation agencies, the Global Accreditation Bureau and the Accreditation Panel for Online Colleges and Universities. However, those accreditation agencies were also listed as fraudulent by retired FBI agent Allen Ezell in his article, "Recent Developments With Degree Mills" published in the educational journal, *College and University*. Many diploma and accreditation mills, including "Corllins University," were also listed. The spelling of Corllins listed in the article does not exactly match the spelling of the university provided by Robertson. Also, search results on the Council for Higher Education Accreditation's (CHEA) database found "Pittsburg State University" and "University of Kansas." A search for "Corllins University" returned no results. CHEA is used by colleges and universities to verify accreditation. "When I went [to Corllins], it was an accredited university," Robertson said. "Otherwise, you can't get any degree authenticated." During the conference call interview, Brown said, "I think [Corllins University] lost its accreditation at some point." In an email to *The Booster*, Robertson also said she had a teacher certification from the University of Cambridge UK. The University of Cambridge confirmed that they offer that degree. Also during the conference call interview, Robertson said she received a bachelor's of fine arts (BFA) in theater arts from the University of Tulsa (UT) in 1991. *The Booster* continued to fact check Robertson's education and contacted UT. According to the registrar's office, a BFA has never been offered at the institution. The university was specific in the degrees offered; only a bachelor of arts in theater was available at that time, not a BFA.

10 After the conference call interview, Brown stated that assistant superintendent Ronda Fincher would serve as the principal of record for the 2017-2018 school year because Robertson currently does not hold a Kansas administrator's license. According to Robertson's contract approved by the USD 250 school board, an "administrator must be licensed in Kansas by August 1, 2018." Whether she can attain a teaching or administrator's license by August 2018 to become an administrator is still in question. According to Brown, she must complete a number of college credit hours to obtain her licensure.

Local Reaction

11 Over the past two weeks, the *The Morning Sun* has also covered questions about Robertson's hiring.

12 On March 20, *The Morning Sun* published a story about Robertson's questioned qualifications inspired by an anonymous letter sent by "Pittsburg Citizen X." PHS band director Cooper Neil responded in *The Morning Sun* Tuesday with a letter to the editor addressing a lack of evidence in the original article. Chance

Copyright © BookheadEd Learning, LLC

Please note that excerpts and passages in the StudySync® library and this workbook are intended as touchstones to generate interest in an author's work. The excerpts and passages do not substitute for the reading of entire texts, and StudySync® strongly recommends that students seek out and purchase the whole literary or informational work in order to experience it as the author intended. Links to online resellers are available in our digital library. In addition, complete works may be ordered through an authorized reseller by filling out and returning to StudySync® the order form enclosed in this workbook.

NOTES

Hoener, the original author, published a response on Wednesday apologizing for failing "to bring closure to . . . rumors via the facts." On Thursday, Pittsburg Community Schools Public Relations director Zach Fletcher issued a press release detailing Robertson's prior professional experience.

13 "When talking with previous supervisors and Dr. Robertson, the Board felt she was a great fit for PHS and the future of our students," Brown, the superintendent, said in the press release. "The high school staff and students who sat in on interviews also felt she was the right pick. We are excited to have her join our team of administrators."

14 In an interview with *The Booster*, French teacher Chris Colyer expressed reservations regarding Robertson. "It concerns me a lot as to how she's going to take all the classes she needs because she's going to have a lot of duties as principal, and that's a full time, and overtime, job," Colyer said. "The fact that she has never taught in a US school does concern me because our schools are different from what she [found] in Dubai." Marjorie Giffin teaches history and social studies at PHS and served on the interview committee for the new principal. "I thought she interviewed very well," Giffin said in an interview with *The Booster*, in reference to Robertson's interview with the committee. "I thought she had all the answers."

15 Brown held a faculty meeting March 17 to address administrative changes, which ended up raising questions for Giffin. "[The meeting] made me more uneasy after than it had before," Giffin continued. "The more [Brown] talked about making us feel at ease about the process made me more worried because I didn't know she wasn't really accredited." "I want some real leadership and I am hoping she can provide it," Giffin said. "I want her to be successful because I want [the school] to get back on track." According to the contract, Robertson begins work at the district July 1.

© 2017 by The Booster Redux Staff. Reproduced by permission of The Booster Redux, c/o Emily Smith.

 WRITE

RHETORICAL ANALYSIS: Select two or three pieces of evidence presented in the article that you found particularly convincing, and explain why you think the evidence is strong. Use details from the text and your knowledge about reasons and evidence to support your response.

Please note that excerpts and passages in the StudySync® library and this workbook are intended as touchstones to generate interest in an author's work. The excerpts and passages do not substitute for the reading of entire texts, and StudySync® strongly recommends that students seek out and purchase the whole literary or informational work in order to experience it as the author intended. Links to online resellers are available in our digital library. In addition, complete works may be ordered through an authorized reseller by filling out and returning to StudySync® the order form enclosed in this workbook.

Copyright © BookheadEd Learning, LLC

Blast: Saving Smart

How will you finance your future?

ⓘ BACKGROUND

Listen to the What's Next podcast associated with this Blast in your digital account.

You may have worked a summer job or earn an allowance for doing chores around the house. You could have chosen to spend a portion of that money to go see a movie or buy a video game, or perhaps you saved up for something more expensive. After high school, you'll still be making similar choices, but with additional expenses to account for, like rent, transportation, insurance and groceries.

The impact and total cost of those expenses depends first and foremost on whether you want to go to college. It also depends on which schools you're deciding between. Community college is typically the most affordable option. The sticker price of an in-state public school is lower than an out-of-state public school or a private school, according to CNBC news. Applying for merit-based or financial scholarship and grants can help to ease the high costs of higher education. You do not need to repay scholarships and grants.

For many college students and their families, however, even a scholarship isn't enough to cover the cost. This is where student loans typically enter the picture. Student loans can help to pay for college. These loans can also be difficult to manage. "Over 44 million Americans collectively hold nearly $1.5 trillion in student debt," a February 2018 CNBC article reports. "That means that roughly one in four American adults are paying off student loans."

Copyright © BookheadEd Learning, LLC

Please note that excerpts and passages in the StudySync® library and this workbook are intended as touchstones to generate interest in an author's work. The excerpts and passages do not substitute for the reading of entire texts, and StudySync® strongly recommends that students seek out and purchase the whole literary or informational work in order to experience it as the author intended. Links to online resellers are available in our digital library. In addition, complete works may be ordered through an authorized reseller by filling out and returning to StudySync® the order form enclosed in this workbook.

NOTES

Some student loans are more manageable than others. Subsidized options, for instance, don't gather interest while you're in college, and have generally lower interest rates after college. This is because the federal government helps to keep costs down, according to Forbes magazine. Unsubsidized loans, on the other hand, do gather interest while you're still in school. This means you will eventually need to pay more than your original loan amount.

Another step after graduating high school may be applying for a credit card. "Credit cards provide an easy opportunity to build credit, which is important when it's time to buy a car or a house," writer Lindsay Konsko says.

However, there are drawbacks to credit cards. Like student loans, you have to carefully read the fine print of the terms. Otherwise, you run the risk of getting stuck with high interest rates. Mark Munzenberger is a financial education specialist. "Obtaining a credit card . . . can be a great way for a young person to establish a good credit history, provided that all payments are made on time and that balances are kept low," Munzenberger told the Detroit Free Press. "Only charge what you can afford to pay off in one month, no matter what," Konsko says. "This is easier to do if you're carefully tracking your spending and keeping it in line with your income."

Assessing the risks associated with student loans and credit cards is part of a longer-term outlook about your financial future. However, the short-term matters, too. Gaby Dunn is the host of the personal finance podcast "Bad with Money." She recommends learning how to budget while in high school. "Now is the least expenses you'll ever have," Dunn says. "You're only making money at this point. That will end very soon."

What do you think? If you plan on going to college, how do you plan to finance it? How long do you think young people should wait to get a credit card? How much do you know about budgeting? How will you finance your future?

NUMBER CRUNCH

37,172

Copyright © BookheadEd Learning, LLC

Please note that excerpts and passages in the StudySync® library and this workbook are intended as touchstones to generate interest in an author's work. The excerpts and passages do not substitute for the reading of entire texts, and StudySync® strongly recommends that students seek out and purchase the whole literary or informational work in order to experience it as the author intended. Links to online resellers are available in our digital library. In addition, complete works may be ordered through an authorized reseller by filling out and returning to StudySync® the order form enclosed in this workbook.

QUIKPOLL

Which of the following is the most important financial decision for a high school graduate to make?

☐ Deciding whether to go to college or get a full-time job

☐ Deciding whether to acquire a credit card

☐ Coming up with a weekly budget and sticking to it

☐ Plotting out how much student loan debt you're willing to take on

CREATE YOUR BLAST

How will you finance your future?

_____

_____

_____

_____

Copyright © BookheadEd Learning, LLC

Please note that excerpts and passages in the StudySync® library and this workbook are intended as touchstones to generate interest in an author's work. The excerpts and passages do not substitute for the reading of entire texts, and StudySync® strongly recommends that students seek out and purchase the whole literary or informational work in order to experience it as the author intended. Links to online resellers are available in our digital library. In addition, complete works may be ordered through an authorized reseller by filling out and returning to StudySync® the order form enclosed in this workbook.

Reading & Writing
Companion   **117**

Blast: Choices, Choices

How will you decide what your future holds?

ⓘ BACKGROUND

Listen to the What's Next podcast associated with this Blast in your digital account.

When you imagine choosing a single path for your life after college, how do you react?

If you get nervous at the idea of making a decision about your future life path, you are not alone. Your life after high school could involve college, a career, travel or any number of options. Deciding on one can seem intimidating. However, author Mike Whitaker believes it is important to learn how to make strategic decisions. "Decisions are forks in the road," Whitaker told Fast Company. "Life doesn't happen to us; we are an active participant. We get out of life what we choose."

People who struggle with decisions may experience a fear of loss, according to psychologist Daniel Kahneman. He says that this is due to loss aversion. This is a difference in value between wins and losses. His research suggests that loss aversion is influential in decision making. "In my classes, I say: 'I'm going to toss a coin, and if it's tails, you lose $10," Kahneman says in a 2013 interview. "How much would you have to gain on winning in order for this gamble to be acceptable to you?'" He says that, on average, people will only accept the gamble if they can win $20 or more. This means that people are willing to lose more money to avoid losing. "People really discriminate sharply between gaining and losing and they don't like losing," Kahneman says.

Copyright © BookheadEd Learning, LLC

Please note that excerpts and passages in the StudySync® library and this workbook are intended as touchstones to generate interest in an author's work. The excerpts and passages do not substitute for the reading of entire texts, and StudySync® strongly recommends that students seek out and purchase the whole literary or informational work in order to experience it as the author intended. Links to online resellers are available in our digital library. In addition, complete works may be ordered through an authorized reseller by filling out and returning to StudySync® the order form enclosed in this workbook.

So, how can you get over that fear of making the wrong life decision? Writers Kate Douglas and Dan Jones argue that most decisions have a much smaller impact than you believe. "Remember also that whatever the future holds, it will probably hurt or please you less than you imagine," Douglas and Jones write in magazine New Scientist.

Writer Elaina Giolando believes that you should think about your motivations. She recommends asking yourself two questions. "Am I doing this because I really want to, or because it would look good," she asked in Fortune. "Am I doing this because I'm just too scared to say no?" Giolando says that these questions can help you to figure out what makes you lean towards one choice.

Philosopher Ruth Chang says that people commonly fear the unknown in decisions. She thinks this fear relies on a misunderstanding of hard choices. "Hard choices are hard not because of us or our ignorance; they're hard because there is no best option," Chang says in a 2014 TEDSalon speech.

There are no best decisions in a lot of scenarios. One example is choosing a college. This choice requires you to consider a lot of different factors. The importance of these factors is different for everyone. You may have to weigh factors like the school's location, tuition and social life. Mike Myatt is a leadership advisor with N2Growth. Myatt says that you should consider four sources of information when making a choice. He ranks these sources from least to most important: gut instincts, data, information and knowledge. Myatt believes that gut instincts can be unreliable. However, he says that instincts can provide a gut check against biased sources. Knowledge, on the other hand, "is information that has been refined by analysis such that it has been assimilated, tested and/or validated," Myatt said.

In the end, Chang says that hard decisions help you shape your identity. She says that hard choices are opportunities. Choices are not always correct or incorrect. When we have a hard choice to make, "we have the power to create reasons for ourselves to become the distinctive people that we are," Chang says.

So, what do you think? How do you typically make decisions? How can you improve your decision-making process? How will you decide what your future holds?

NUMBER CRUNCH

2014

Copyright © BookheadEd Learning, LLC

Please note that excerpts and passages in the StudySync® library and this workbook are intended as touchstones to generate interest in an author's work. The excerpts and passages do not substitute for the reading of entire texts, and StudySync® strongly recommends that students seek out and purchase the whole literary or informational work in order to experience it as the author intended. Links to online resellers are available in our digital library. In addition, complete works may be ordered through an authorized reseller by filling out and returning to StudySync® the order form enclosed in this workbook.

Reading & Writing Companion 119

NOTES

QUIKPOLL

Is it typically easy for you to make a decision?

☐ Yes. It's easy to make decisions because I can always weigh my options and pick one.

☐ Sometimes. I don't always make decisions easily, but I don't agonize over most decisions.

☐ No. It's really hard for me to make decisions, because it always seems like I have too many options.

✶ CREATE YOUR BLAST

How will you decide what your future holds?

_____

_____

_____

_____

Please note that excerpts and passages in the StudySync® library and this workbook are intended as touchstones to generate interest in an author's work. The excerpts and passages do not substitute for the reading of entire texts, and StudySync® strongly recommends that students seek out and purchase the whole literary or informational work in order to experience it as the author intended. Links to online resellers are available in our digital library. In addition, complete works may be ordered through an authorized reseller by filling out and returning to StudySync® the order form enclosed in this workbook.

Copyright © BookheadEd Learning, LLC

Blast: Going Forth

What should all high schoolers know?

Copyright © BookheadEd Learning, LLC

BACKGROUND

Listen to the What's Next podcast associated with this Blast in your digital account.

Senior year of high school is a time of mixed emotions — joy and exhaustion, pride and regret, excitement and anxiety. As you navigate big decisions at the end of high school, chances are you'll reflect on where you've been, where you are, and where you're going.

This was a common experience for the students featured in StudySync's "What's Next?" Blast and podcast series. Students looked back at their senior year and realized how their perspectives had changed and how they'd grown as people.

For some students — like Kiana Griffin — plans for life after high school changed drastically over the course of nine months. At the beginning of the school year, Griffin expected to go to a four-year D1 university to play basketball on a full scholarship. However, a knee injury forced her to consider different options, and she ultimately went with a community college.

For other students — like DJ Frost — their mindset remained consistent all year. Frost had his post-grad plan locked in before his senior year began. So, he spent the year focusing on solidifying friendships, finishing academically strong and preparing for the year ahead.

Listen to the final podcast in the "What's Next?" series. Then, read about each student's final plans below:

Please note that excerpts and passages in the StudySync® library and this workbook are intended as touchstones to generate interest in an author's work. The excerpts and passages do not substitute for the reading of entire texts, and StudySync® strongly recommends that students seek out and purchase the whole literary or informational work in order to experience it as the author intended. Links to online resellers are available in our digital library. In addition, complete works may be ordered through an authorized reseller by filling out and returning to StudySync® the order form enclosed in this workbook.

NOTES

Diana-Nicole Ramirez will attend Adelphi University on Long Island, New York to study journalism and communications. In the spring, a rejection letter from New York University devastated Diana-Nicole. However, when she visited Adelphi, she fell in love. She says her senior year made her a more positive person.

DJ Frost will attend the Air Force Academy in Colorado to play football and major in business. Since his decision was made before his senior year began, DJ focused on finishing strong and looking ahead. DJ said his goal is to "become the best me that I can be while helping as many people as I can."

Felicia Horn will attend Fairfield University in Connecticut to study nursing. Eventually, she wants to become a nurse anesthetist. Felicia got deferred from Fairfield University initially, but she wrote the school expressing her interest and conducted an interview with the admissions team. She got accepted. In April, she struggled to decide between Fairfield University and Sacred Heart University. In the end, she chose Fairfield because it had more name recognition and her gut said it was the better choice.

Katherine Carlo will attend the University of Florida on a full scholarship. She doesn't know what she wants to study yet, but she's starting with classes in business. Katherine applied to prestigious universities and scholarships throughout the East Coast. When she got rejected from some of the bigger scholarships she applied to, and learned she would have merit-based financial aid at UF, she knew the school was the right move for her.

Kiana Griffin will attend Sacramento City College to play basketball, in hopes of one day transferring to a four-year university to play D1. After her injury and surgery, Kiana decided that community college was the best decision directly out of high school. Once she heals and can play to her full potential again, she hopes to build back her basketball career and transfer to a larger school.

Lyssa Nix will attend Bellus Academy, a cosmetology school in San Diego, and join their esthetician program. Lyssa knew from the beginning of the year that she wanted to pursue being an esthetician. However, she wasn't sure where she wanted to go or how to apply. After touring schools and talking to mentors, she's preparing to start a program she's excited about.

Makalya Adams will attend Hinds Community College in Jackson, Mississippi, where she hopes to get prerequisite credits before transferring to nursing school. Makalya had a good feeling about Hinds Community College from the beginning, but her mom pushed back. Her mom wanted her to go to a private university. However, Makalya knew she should make the decision that felt right to her, and she's proud that she made that decision on her own.

Copyright © BookheadEd Learning, LLC

Please note that excerpts and passages in the StudySync® library and this workbook are intended as touchstones to generate interest in an author's work. The excerpts and passages do not substitute for the reading of entire texts, and StudySync® strongly recommends that students seek out and purchase the whole literary or informational work in order to experience it as the author intended. Links to online resellers are available in our digital library. In addition, complete works may be ordered through an authorized reseller by filling out and returning to StudySync® the order form enclosed in this workbook.

Patrick Cadogan will begin his senior in high school at Westford Academy in Westford, Massachusetts. Patrick began the year wanting to go to college close to home, but after touring a few schools further away, he's opened his mind to more options. After taking the SAT this year, he's ready to get started on college applications over the summer.

Shamora Rogers will attend Stephen F. Austin University in Nacogdoches, Texas to study theater, film and television. Shamora prioritized a strong theater program and affordability when she applied to college. Those priorities helped her choose Stephen F. Austin University in the end. Financial aid will help her pay for school, and she's still waiting to hear back from various outside scholarships as well.

Zac Walsdorf will attend Notre Dame University in South Bend, Indiana and study psychology. After getting rejected from several of his top choices, Zac narrowed down his college choices to his state school and Notre Dame University. When he visited Notre Dame and met some of the other students, he knew he could make it his home for four years.

As you've seen and heard, the students we interviewed are moving into their adult lives with all kinds of different mindsets, goals and road maps. But they're all graduating with insights and advice for other students going through the same things.

What do you think? What did you learn from the students featured in the "What's Next?" podcast series? What do you think every student should keep in mind during their senior year? How will you make your last year of high school count? What should all high schoolers know?

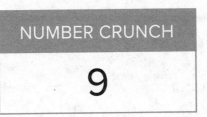

NUMBER CRUNCH

9

Copyright © BookheadEd Learning, LLC

Please note that excerpts and passages in the StudySync® library and this workbook are intended as touchstones to generate interest in an author's work. The excerpts and passages do not substitute for the reading of entire texts, and StudySync® strongly recommends that students seek out and purchase the whole literary or informational work in order to experience it as the author intended. Links to online resellers are available in our digital library. In addition, complete works may be ordered through an authorized reseller by filling out and returning to StudySync® the order form enclosed in this workbook.

Reading & Writing Companion   **123**

NOTES

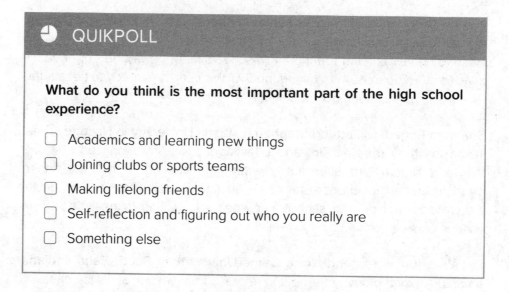

QUIKPOLL

What do you think is the most important part of the high school experience?

- ☐ Academics and learning new things
- ☐ Joining clubs or sports teams
- ☐ Making lifelong friends
- ☐ Self-reflection and figuring out who you really are
- ☐ Something else

✴ CREATE YOUR BLAST

What should all high schoolers know?

_____

_____

_____

_____

Please note that excerpts and passages in the StudySync® library and this workbook are intended as touchstones to generate interest in an author's work. The excerpts and passages do not substitute for the reading of entire texts, and StudySync® strongly recommends that students seek out and purchase the whole literary or informational work in order to experience it as the author intended. Links to online resellers are available in our digital library. In addition, complete works may be ordered through an authorized reseller by filling out and returning to StudySync® the order form enclosed in this workbook.

Copyright © BookheadEd Learning, LLC

Extended Writing Project and Grammar

EXTENDED WRITING PROJECT
INFORMATIVE WRITING

Informative Writing Process: Plan

PLAN	DRAFT	REVISE	EDIT AND PUBLISH

Humans are complex beings, shaped by the many facets of life. Born with incredibly similar genetic material, we develop into strikingly different personalities with singular, often divergent goals. These goals, shaped by our past, guide us into the future and into the ways we will transform this world.

WRITING PROMPT

How will our understanding of who we are shape the goals we develop for ourselves?

Reflect on your background, identity, interests, and talents. Think through experiences you have had and obstacles you have faced. Which of these aspects of life have had the greatest impact on who you are now? Select two to four of these aspects. Describe what you learned from them, how you developed as a result of them, and how they affect the goals you are setting for your future self. Your personal essay should include the following:

- a strong thesis statement
- an introduction
- a clear organizational structure
- supporting details
- a conclusion

Copyright © BookheadEd Learning, LLC

Please note that excerpts and passages in the StudySync® library and this workbook are intended as touchstones to generate interest in an author's work. The excerpts and passages do not substitute for the reading of entire texts, and StudySync® strongly recommends that students seek out and purchase the whole literary or informational work in order to experience it as the author intended. Links to online resellers are available in our digital library. In addition, complete works may be ordered through an authorized reseller by filling out and returning to StudySync® the order form enclosed in this workbook.

Introduction to Informative Writing

Informative writing includes a main idea or thesis statement that focuses on a particular aspect of a topic. Informative texts use evidence—such as definitions, quotations, examples, and facts—that clarifies and supports the thesis statement. In personal essays, authors use many of the attributes used in informative writing, but they also use anecdotes and commentary on actual events to support their thesis statement. However, the purpose of informative writing is to inform readers about real people, places, things, and events, so authors of personal essays still need to organize their ideas, concepts, and information in a logical way.

Writers carefully choose an organizational structure, such as definition, classification, compare/contrast, or cause and effect, that best suits their material. Often, informative writing includes visual elements such as headings, graphics, and/or tables to communicate complex ideas or information. The characteristics of informative writing include:

- an introduction with a clear thesis statement
- a clear and logical organizational structure that includes supporting details
- transitions that link sections of text and support the organization of complex ideas
- precise language and a formal or informal style appropriate to the topic
- a conclusion that unifies ideas

Writers also carefully craft their work so that each new element builds on that which precedes it to create a unified whole. In a personal essay, authors often have a more subjective point of view and informal style that readers can easily identify. Effective personal essays combine these informative genre characteristics and craft to engage the reader.

As you continue with this Extended Writing Project, you'll receive more instruction and practice in crafting each of the characteristics of informative writing to create your own personal essay.

Copyright © BookheadEd Learning, LLC

Please note that excerpts and passages in the StudySync® library and this workbook are intended as touchstones to generate interest in an author's work. The excerpts and passages do not substitute for the reading of entire texts, and StudySync® strongly recommends that students seek out and purchase the whole literary or informational work in order to experience it as the author intended. Links to online resellers are available in our digital library. In addition, complete works may be ordered through an authorized reseller by filling out and returning to StudySync® the order form enclosed in this workbook.

Reading & Writing
Companion

127

Before you get started on your own personal essay, read this personal essay that one student, Monica, wrote in response to the writing prompt. As you read the Model, highlight and annotate the features of informative writing that Monica included in her personal essay.

☰ STUDENT MODEL

My So-Called Introverted Life

1   When you look in the mirror, what do you see? I see dark brown hair, hazel eyes, and a somewhat crooked smile. Beneath the surface, though, I see a loyal heart, fierce determination, and an introverted personality. Those are the things that make me Monica, but I haven't always appreciated the qualities that make me *me*. Since I grew up in a loud, gregarious family, I always thought something was wrong with me because I didn't want to spend all of my time around other people, especially new people. My family seemed to agree and would shake their heads when I tried to get away from the noise on holidays. During my junior year of high school, however, I learned that being different doesn't mean I'm flawed. Sometimes the qualities that others consider to be your greatest weaknesses turn out to be your greatest strengths.

Background and Identity

2   School work has always come easy to me. Making new friends has not. My teachers praised my talent for language but always noted that I am uncomfortable working in groups, especially if my best friend wasn't also involved. Kayla and I have been inseparable since elementary school. We were assigned to share a cubby in first grade, and we've been partners ever since. My family warned me against forming such a close attachment with just one friend. What would happen if the relationship fell apart? I stubbornly refused to seek other companions. My friendship with Kayla always felt like a safety net. With Kayla, I could always be myself. She understood if I needed space and encouraged me to take care of myself. It felt disloyal to look for other friends when Kayla gave me all the support I needed. As we grew older, though, we started growing apart. Although Kayla and I have always been extremely close—our classmates even jokingly referred to us as "Kaylica"—we are also very different. Kayla is friendly and outgoing, while I am more reserved. She loves science

Please note that excerpts and passages in the StudySync® library and this workbook are intended as touchstones to generate interest in an author's work. The excerpts and passages do not substitute for the reading of entire texts, and StudySync® strongly recommends that students seek out and purchase the whole literary or informational work in order to experience it as the author intended. Links to online resellers are available in our digital library. In addition, complete works may be ordered through an authorized reseller by filling out and returning to StudySync® the order form enclosed in this workbook.

Copyright © BookheadEd Learning, LLC

and working in the community garden on weekends, but I'd much rather curl up with a good book or write a short story. Last year, Kayla's aptitude in science led her to apply to a STEM program at a local private high school. She was accepted, and while I was thrilled for her, I was overwhelmed by the idea of having to begin a new school year without my best friend by my side.

Interests and Talents

3   The first days of junior year were hard. Although I enjoy being by myself, the school day can feel incredibly long if you have no one else to talk to. Each night, Kayla would call to tell me about the new friends she was making and the new adventures she was having. My heart sank as I realized she was thriving without me. My family's criticism of my introversion and stubborn insistence to remain loyal to a single friend came flooding back. I'd never felt so alone. That's when I made a decision. Like Kayla, I needed to find a new group who shared my interests and who would accept me for who I am.

4   The school's newspaper seemed like a natural fit, so I signed up. I'd thought about joining the paper before but was intimidated by the newsrooms I'd seen on television and in movies. If I can't handle Sunday night dinner with my extended family, how was I supposed to work amid the hustle and bustle of such a high-stakes environment? After I dragged myself to my first newspaper meeting, though, I quickly realized how silly I had been. The newspaper office was actually small and unintimidating. Four students sat at computers, silently working on their own individual assignments. When I walked in, they looked up and offered small smiles before returning their eyes to their screens. These students were all part of the same team, working toward a shared goal, but they were doing so at their own pace and in their own spaces. It was perfect for me.

Self-Acceptance

5   In the following weeks, I began to look forward to newspaper meetings as much as I looked forward to my nightly calls with Kayla. My assignments were tough, especially when I had to interview strangers for a story. Yet my determination to succeed kept me focused, and knowing that I planned to spend time alone to write about each new experience kept me motivated. I also developed strong feelings of loyalty toward the newspaper staff. They might not

Copyright © BookheadEd Learning, LLC

Please note that excerpts and passages in the StudySync® library and this workbook are intended as touchstones to generate interest in an author's work. The excerpts and passages do not substitute for the reading of entire texts, and StudySync® strongly recommends that students seek out and purchase the whole literary or informational work in order to experience it as the author intended. Links to online resellers are available in our digital library. In addition, complete works may be ordered through an authorized reseller by filling out and returning to StudySync® the order form enclosed in this workbook.

be my best friends, but they were my new team. With each passing day, it became clearer that I didn't have to change who I am in order to be happy. My loyalty, determination, and introverted personality might not be the best qualities in every situation, but it turned out that they are the perfect recipe for a reporter. Before I walked into the newspaper office, I had no idea what I wanted to do after graduation, but now I know. I want to study journalism and become a correspondent for a newspaper.

6   Facing the world without Kayla always by my side was scarier than a proud introvert like me would like to admit, but I am grateful that I went through the difficult experience. It showed me that my loyal heart, fierce determination, and introverted personality could be assets for my future. Instead of causing me to be alone and unengaged, my personality can actually help me connect with others because the way I see the world helps me write stories about the world. Now that I know this, when I cross the stage at graduation, I believe that I'll have the confidence to pursue a bright future on my own.

Please note that excerpts and passages in the StudySync® library and this workbook are intended as touchstones to generate interest in an author's work. The excerpts and passages do not substitute for the reading of entire texts, and StudySync® strongly recommends that students seek out and purchase the whole literary or informational work in order to experience it as the author intended. Links to online resellers are available in our digital library. In addition, complete works may be ordered through an authorized reseller by filling out and returning to StudySync® the order form enclosed in this workbook.

Copyright © BookheadEd Learning, LLC

✏️ WRITE

Writers often take notes about their ideas before they sit down to write. Think about what you've learned so far about organizing informative writing to help you begin prewriting.

- **Purpose:** How do you see yourself? What experiences had the greatest impact on who you are now?
- **Audience:** Who is your audience, and how might your audience connect to your essay? How will you engage your audience?
- **Introduction:** How will you clearly introduce the topic and the main idea of your essay? What language can you use that is both personal and intriguing?
- **Thesis Statement:** How did your experiences affect you? What two to four aspects of life have had the greatest impact on you?
- **Organizational Text Structure:** What strategies will you use to organize your response to the prompt? Will you explain your experiences chronologically or by ideas?
- **Evidence, Examples, and Anecdotes:** What evidence or examples relate to your thesis? What anecdotes exemplify your ideas?
- **Conclusion:** How does the information in the body of your essay relate to your thesis? How can you connect the ideas in your personal essay to your audience or to a larger idea about society?

Response Instructions

Use the questions in the bulleted list to write a one-paragraph summary. Your summary should describe what you will explain in your personal essay.

Don't worry about including all of the details now; focus only on the most essential and important elements. You will refer to this short summary as you continue through the steps of the writing process.

Copyright © BookheadEd Learning, LLC

Please note that excerpts and passages in the StudySync® library and this workbook are intended as touchstones to generate interest in an author's work. The excerpts and passages do not substitute for the reading of entire texts, and StudySync® strongly recommends that students seek out and purchase the whole literary or informational work in order to experience it as the author intended. Links to online resellers are available in our digital library. In addition, complete works may be ordered through an authorized reseller by filling out and returning to StudySync® the order form enclosed in this workbook.

Skill:
Organizing Informative Writing

••• CHECKLIST FOR ORGANIZING INFORMATIVE WRITING

As you begin to organize your writing for your informative essay, use the following questions as a guide:

- What is a brief summary of my topic?

- How can I organize my ideas so that each new element builds on previous material?

- Can I use visual elements, such as headings, to organize my essay by dividing information into sections?

Here are steps you can use to organize complex ideas, concepts, and information so that each new element builds on that which precedes it to create a unified whole:

- definitions

  > first, define a subject or concept

  > second, define the qualities of the subject or concept

  > third, provide examples, focusing on showing different aspects of the subject or concept

- categories

  > first, identify the main idea or topic

  > second, divide the main idea or topic into categories, focusing on how you want to explain your ideas

  > third, use the categories to provide descriptive details and deepen your reader's understanding

- comparisons

  > first, identify two texts about similar topics to compare

  > second, identify the similarities and differences between the texts

  > third, determine how those comparisons reveal larger ideas about the topic of the texts

- cause and effect

  > first, determine what happened in a text, including the order of events

  > second, identify the reasons that something happened

  > third, connect what happened and the reasons for it to the main idea or claim

Copyright © BookheadEd Learning, LLC

Please note that excerpts and passages in the StudySync® library and this workbook are intended as touchstones to generate interest in an author's work. The excerpts and passages do not substitute for the reading of entire texts, and StudySync® strongly recommends that students seek out and purchase the whole literary or informational work in order to experience it as the author intended. Links to online resellers are available in our digital library. In addition, complete works may be ordered through an authorized reseller by filling out and returning to StudySync® the order form enclosed in this workbook.

⟳ YOUR TURN

Read the statements in the first column in the chart below. Then, in the second column, write the corresponding letter for the organizational structure that would be most appropriate for the purpose and topic of each statement.

Organizational Structure Options	
A	Compare and contrast
B	Advantages and disadvantages
C	Definition or classification
D	Categories and subcategories
E	Cause and effect

Statement	Organizational Structure
Kayla's aptitude in science led her to apply to a STEM program.	
Sometimes the qualities that others consider to be your greatest weaknesses turn out to be your greatest strengths.	
Although Kayla and I have always been extremely close—our classmates even jokingly referred to us as "Kaylica"—we are also very different.	
During my junior year of high school, however, I learned that being different doesn't mean I'm flawed.	
Beneath the surface, though, I see a loyal heart, fierce determination, and an introverted personality. Those are the things that make me Monica, but I haven't always appreciated the qualities that make me *me*.	

Copyright © BookheadEd Learning, LLC

Please note that excerpts and passages in the StudySync® library and this workbook are intended as touchstones to generate interest in an author's work. The excerpts and passages do not substitute for the reading of entire texts, and StudySync® strongly recommends that students seek out and purchase the whole literary or informational work in order to experience it as the author intended. Links to online resellers are available in our digital library. In addition, complete works may be ordered through an authorized reseller by filling out and returning to StudySync® the order form enclosed in this workbook.

YOUR TURN

Complete the chart below by writing key ideas to include in each paragraph of your essay.

Paragraph	Key Idea
Introduction	
Body Paragraph 1	
Body Paragraph 2	
Body Paragraph 3	
Conclusion	

Copyright © BookheadEd Learning, LLC

Please note that excerpts and passages in the StudySync® library and this workbook are intended as touchstones to generate interest in an author's work. The excerpts and passages do not substitute for the reading of entire texts, and StudySync® strongly recommends that students seek out and purchase the whole literary or informational work in order to experience it as the author intended. Links to online resellers are available in our digital library. In addition, complete works may be ordered through an authorized reseller by filling out and returning to StudySync® the order form enclosed in this workbook.

Skill:
Thesis Statement

••• CHECKLIST FOR THESIS STATEMENT

Before you begin writing your thesis statement, ask yourself the following questions:

- What is the prompt asking me to write about?
- What claim do I want to make about the topic of this essay?
- Is my claim precise and informative? How is it specific to my topic? How does it inform the reader about my topic?
- Does my thesis statement introduce the body of my essay?
- Where should I place my thesis statement?

Here are some steps for introducing and developing a topic as well as a precise and informative claim:

- think about your central claim of your essay
  - > identify a clear claim you want to introduce, thinking about:
    - o how closely your claim is related to your topic and how specific it is to your supporting details
    - o how your claim includes necessary information to guide the reader through the topic
- your thesis statement should:
  - > let the reader anticipate the content of your essay
  - > help you begin your essay in an organized manner
  - > present your opinion clearly
  - > respond completely to the writing prompt
- consider the best placement for your thesis statement
  - > if your response is short, you may want to get right to the point and present your thesis statement in the first sentence of the essay
  - > if your response is longer (as in a formal essay), you can build up to your thesis statement and place it at the end of your introductory paragraph

Please note that excerpts and passages in the StudySync® library and this workbook are intended as touchstones to generate interest in an author's work. The excerpts and passages do not substitute for the reading of entire texts, and StudySync® strongly recommends that students seek out and purchase the whole literary or informational work in order to experience it as the author intended. Links to online resellers are available in our digital library. In addition, complete works may be ordered through an authorized reseller by filling out and returning to StudySync® the order form enclosed in this workbook.

Copyright © BookheadEd Learning, LLC

↻ YOUR TURN

Read the statements below. Then, complete the chart by sorting the statements into two categories: thesis statements and details. Write the corresponding letter for each statement in the appropriate column.

	Statement Options
A	I prefer to keep to myself, but at the same time my friends know that I am loyal.
B	I am someone who prefers to read a book than socialize with a large group of people.
C	Although some people consider my shy personality a weakness, I consider it a strength.
D	It turned out that those qualities are the perfect recipe for a reporter.
E	Sometimes our personalities just need the right context in which to flourish.
F	All of my characteristics, both the positive and the negative, are what make me a strong person.

Thesis Statement	Details

✎ WRITE

Use the checklist to draft a thesis statement for your personal essay.

Please note that excerpts and passages in the StudySync® library and this workbook are intended as touchstones to generate interest in an author's work. The excerpts and passages do not substitute for the reading of entire texts, and StudySync® strongly recommends that students seek out and purchase the whole literary or informational work in order to experience it as the author intended. Links to online resellers are available in our digital library. In addition, complete works may be ordered through an authorized reseller by filling out and returning to StudySync® the order form enclosed in this workbook.

Copyright © BookheadEd Learning, LLC

Skill:
Supporting Details

••• CHECKLIST FOR SUPPORTING DETAILS

As you look for supporting details to develop your topic, claim, or thesis statement, ask yourself the following questions:

*   What is my main idea about this topic?

*   What does a reader need to know about the topic in order to understand the main idea?

*   What details will support my thesis?

*   What other kinds of information could I provide?

*   Does this information help to develop and refine my main idea?

*   Does this information relate closely to my thesis or claim?

*   Are the supporting details I have included sufficient to support my thesis or claim?

Here are some suggestions for how you can develop your topic:

*   review your thesis or claim

*   consider what your audience may already know about the topic

*   note what the audience will need to know to understand the topic

*   develop your topic thoroughly and accurately, taking into consideration all of its aspects

*   use different types of supporting details, such as:

    >   the most significant and relevant facts that are specific to your topic, make an impact in your discussion, and fully support your thesis or claim

    >   concrete details that will add descriptive material to your topic

    >   quotations to directly connect your thesis statement or claim to the text

    >   examples and other information to deepen the audience's knowledge

Please note that excerpts and passages in the StudySync® library and this workbook are intended as touchstones to generate interest in an author's work. The excerpts and passages do not substitute for the reading of entire texts, and StudySync® strongly recommends that students seek out and purchase the whole literary or informational work in order to experience it as the author intended. Links to online resellers are available in our digital library. In addition, complete works may be ordered through an authorized reseller by filling out and returning to StudySync® the order form enclosed in this workbook.

Copyright © BookheadEd Learning, LLC

YOUR TURN

Choose the best answer to each question.

The following sentence is from a draft of a student's personal essay on the impact of having parents who speak a different language. Select the supporting detail below that best supports the topic.

> Growing up with parents who speak a language besides English has helped me appreciate the many diverse cultures in our school and community.

○ A. Many students at school only know English, and this makes it hard for us to all get to know each other because many people in our community speak another language at home.

○ B. My parents want me to take Spanish classes at school so I can talk with our neighbors down the street and make friends with their children, who are my age.

○ C. At home, my parents speak Polish, and seeing how they have become close friends with the many diverse people in our neighborhood has encouraged me to be open-minded.

○ D. Do you ever feel like you are the only person who has non-English-speaking parents?

 YOUR TURN

Complete the chart below by listing ideas and relevant supporting details that will help your audience understand these ideas in your essay. The first row presents an example.

Ideas	What the Audience Needs to Know	Supporting Details
Speaking two languages also means you connect with two cultures.	My audience needs to understand how speaking two languages helps you connect with cultures better.	Saying *thanks* in English means that you are "giving thanks" and acknowledgement to someone. In Portuguese, *obrigado* is the way we say "thank you," but it translates as "I am obligated to you." This is just one example of how knowing just one word in each language can help you understand each culture.

Copyright © BookheadEd Learning, LLC

Please note that excerpts and passages in the StudySync® library and this workbook are intended as touchstones to generate interest in an author's work. The excerpts and passages do not substitute for the reading of entire texts, and StudySync® strongly recommends that students seek out and purchase the whole literary or informational work in order to experience it as the author intended. Links to online resellers are available in our digital library. In addition, complete works may be ordered through an authorized reseller by filling out and returning to StudySync® the order form enclosed in this workbook.

Informative Writing Process: Draft

| PLAN | DRAFT | REVISE | EDIT AND PUBLISH |

You have already made progress toward writing your personal essay. Now it is time to draft your personal essay.

✎ WRITE

Use your plan and other responses in your Binder to draft your essay. You may also have new ideas as you begin drafting. Feel free to explore those new ideas as you have them. You can also ask yourself these questions to ensure that your writing is focused, organized, and detailed:

Draft Checklist:

☐ **Purpose and Focus:** Have I made my thesis clear to readers?

☐ **Organization:** Does the organizational structure in my essay make sense? Will readers be interested in the way I present information and my commentary? Does my writing flow together naturally, or is it choppy?

☐ **Ideas and Details:** Will my readers be able to easily follow and understand my ideas? Have I included only relevant examples?

Before you submit your draft, read it over carefully. You want to be sure that you've responded to all aspects of the prompt.

Copyright © BookheadEd Learning, LLC

Please note that excerpts and passages in the StudySync® library and this workbook are intended as touchstones to generate interest in an author's work. The excerpts and passages do not substitute for the reading of entire texts, and StudySync® strongly recommends that students seek out and purchase the whole literary or informational work in order to experience it as the author intended. Links to online resellers are available in our digital library. In addition, complete works may be ordered through an authorized reseller by filling out and returning to StudySync® the order form enclosed in this workbook.

Reading & Writing Companion **139**

Here is Monica's personal essay draft. As you read, notice how Monica develops her draft to be focused, organized, and detailed. As she continues to revise and edit her personal essay, she will improve the style of her writing, as well as correct any grammatical mistakes.

NOTES

Skill:
Introductions

Monica strengthens her introduction by adding a hook. She provides an intriguing question and uses it to describe her appearance and her personality. These changes make her introduction more interesting and better introduce the ideas she will develop in her essay.

☰ STUDENT MODEL: FIRST DRAFT

Weaknesses are Strengths

~~I grew up in a loud family, and I always thought something was wrong with me because I liked being by myself. My family seemed to agree and would shake their heads when I tried to get away from the noise on holidays. During my junior year of high school, however, I learned that being different doesnt mean Im flawed. Parts of my personality used to seem like weaknesses, but later I learned that they were actually my strengths.~~

When you look in the mirror, what do you see? I see dark brown hair, hazel eyes, and a somewhat crooked smile. Beneath the surface, though, I see a loyal heart, fierce determination, and an introverted personality. Those are the things that make me Monica, but I haven't always appreciated the qualities that make me *me*. Since I grew up in a loud, gregarious family, I always thought something was wrong with me because I didn't want to spend all of my time around other people, especially new people. My family seemed to agree and would shake their heads when I tried to get away from the noise on holidays. During my junior year of high school, however, I learned that being different doesn't mean I'm flawed. Sometimes the qualities that others consider to be your greatest weaknesses turn out to be your greatest strengths.

Background and Identity

~~School work has always come easy to me. Making new friends has not. My teachers praised my talent for language but always noted that I am uncomfortable working in groups. Kayla and I have been inseparateable since elementary school. We were assigned to share a cubby in first grade, and weve been partners ever since. My family warned me against forming such a close attachment with just one friend. What would happen if the relationship fell apart? I would not seek other companions. My friend-ship with Kayla always seemed~~

Please note that excerpts and passages in the StudySync® library and this workbook are intended as touchstones to generate interest in an author's work. The excerpts and passages do not substitute for the reading of entire texts, and StudySync® strongly recommends that students seek out and purchase the whole literary or informational work in order to experience it as the author intended. Links to online resellers are available in our digital library. In addition, complete works may be ordered through an authorized reseller by filling out and returning to StudySync® the order form enclosed in this workbook.

Copyright © BookheadEd Learning, LLC

NOTES

friends she was making and the new adventures she was having. My heart sank as I realized she was thriving without me. My familys criticism of my shyness and insistentce to remain close to a single freind came flooding back. Never felt so alone. That's when I made a decision. Like Kayla, I needed to find a new group who shared my interests and who would accept me for who I am.

After I dragged myself to my first newspaper meeting, though, I quickly realized how silly I had been. Id thought about joining the paper before but was intimidated by the newsrooms Id seen on television and in movies. If I cant handle Sunday night dinner with my extended family, how was I supposed to work amid the hustle and bustle of such a high-stakes environment? The school's newspaper seemed like a natural fit, though, so I signed up. The newspaper office was actually small. It was also unintimidating. Four students sat at computers. They silently working on their own invidual assignments. When I walked in, they looked up. They offered small smiles. Then returned their eyes to their screens. These students were all part of the same team and they worked toward a shared goal and they were doing so at their own pace and in their own spaces. It was perfict for me.

Self-Acceptance

In the following weeks, I began to look forward to newspaper meetings. I also looked forward to my nightly calls with Kayla. My assignments were tough. I had to inter view strangers. My desire to succeed kept me focused. I spent time alone to write about each new exspereince. They might not be my best friends, but they were my new team. I also developed strong feelings of commitment toward the newspaper staff. With each passing day, it became clearer that I didnt have to change who I am in order to be happy. My desire to be alone and my shy personality might not be the best qualitys in every situation. It turned out that they are the perfect recipe for a reporter. Before I walked into the newspaper office, I had no idea what I wanted to do after graduation. Now I know. I want to study journalism and become a correspondent for a newspaper.

~~My desire to be a good friend and shy personality can be assets for my future. Sometimes the qualities that others consider to be your greatest weaknesses turn out to be your greatest strengths. Now~~

Copyright © BookheadEd Learning, LLC

Please note that excerpts and passages in the StudySync® library and this workbook are intended as touchstones to generate interest in an author's work. The excerpts and passages do not substitute for the reading of entire texts, and StudySync® strongly recommends that students seek out and purchase the whole literary or informational work in order to experience it as the author intended. Links to online resellers are available in our digital library. In addition, complete works may be ordered through an authorized reseller by filling out and returning to StudySync® the order form enclosed in this workbook.

very important to me and I did not feel as comfortable with anyone else. With Kayla, I could always be myself. She understood if I needed space and let me take care of myself. It didn't feel right to look for other friends when Kayla gave me all the support I needed. As we grew older, though, started growing apart. Kayla and I have always been extremily close. Our classmates even jokingly referred to us as "Kaylica." We are also very different. Kayla is friendly and outgoing while I am more reserved. Last year, Kaylas aptitude in science led her to aply to a STEM program at a local privat high school. She was accepted. I was thrilled for her. I was scared of the idea of having to begin a new school year without my best friend by my side.

School work has always come easy to me. Making new friends has not. My teachers praised my talent for language but always noted that I am uncomfortable working in groups, especially if my best friend wasn't also involved. Kayla and I have been inseparable since elementary school. We were assigned to share a cubby in first grade, and we've been partners ever since. My family warned me against forming such a close attachment with just one friend. What would happen if the relationship fell apart? I stubbornly refused to seek other companions. My friendship with Kayla always felt like a safety net. With Kayla, I could always be myself. She understood if I needed space and encouraged me to take care of myself. It felt disloyal to look for other friends when Kayla gave me all the support I needed. As we grew older, though, we started growing apart. Although Kayla and I have always been extremely close—our classmates even jokingly referred to us as "Kaylica"—we are also very different. Kayla is friendly and outgoing, while I am more reserved. She loves science and working in the community garden on weekends, but I'd much rather curl up with a good book or write a short story. Last year, Kayla's aptitude in science led her to apply to a STEM program at a local private high school. She was accepted, and while I was thrilled for her, I was overwhelmed by the idea of having to begin a new school year without my best friend by my side.

Interests and Talents

The first days of junior year were hard. Although I enjoy being by myself, the school day can feel incredibley long if you have no one else to talk to. Each night, Kayla would call to tell me about the new

Copyright © BookheadEd Learning, LLC

Sk
Pre

Monica r
sentence
ship with
seemed
to me . .
She can
convey t
of their
the impo
absence

Sk
Tr

Monica
transitic
express
contrad
relation
more cl
adds th
at the e
paragro
express
emotion

Please note that excerpts and passages in the StudySync® library and this workbook are intended as touchstones to generate interest in an author's work. The excerpts and passages do not substitute for the reading of entire texts, and StudySync® strongly recommends that students seek out and purchase the whole literary or informational work in order to experience it as the author intended. Links to online resellers are available in our digital library. In addition, complete works may be ordered through an authorized reseller by filling out and returning to StudySync® the order form enclosed in this workbook.

that I know this, when I cross the stage at graduation, I believe that I'll have the confidence to pursue a bright future on my own.

Facing the world without Kayla always by my side was scarier than a proud introvert like me would like to admit, but I am grateful that I went through the difficult experience. It showed me that my loyal heart, fierce determination, and introverted personality could be assets for my future. Instead of causing me to be alone and unengaged, my personality can actually help me connect with others because the way I see the world helps me write stories about the world. Now that I know this, when I cross the stage at graduation, I believe that I'll have the confidence to pursue a bright future on my own.

NOTES

Skill:
Conclusions

Monica strengthens her final paragraph by creating a smoother transition between her body paragraphs and conclusion. She also rephrases her thesis, adding specific details to reinforce the significance of her topic and leave her audience with a memorable idea.

Copyright © BookheadEd Learning, LLC

Please note that excerpts and passages in the StudySync® library and this workbook are intended as touchstones to generate interest in an author's work. The excerpts and passages do not substitute for the reading of entire texts, and StudySync® strongly recommends that students seek out and purchase the whole literary or informational work in order to experience it as the author intended. Links to online resellers are available in our digital library. In addition, complete works may be ordered through an authorized reseller by filling out and returning to StudySync® the order form enclosed in this workbook.

Reading & Writing
Companion

143

Skill:
Introductions

••• CHECKLIST FOR INTRODUCTIONS

Before you write your introduction, ask yourself the following questions:

- What is my claim? In addition:

  > How can I make it more precise and informative?

  > Have I included why my claim is significant to discuss? How does it help the reader understand the topic better?

- How can I introduce my topic? Have I organized complex ideas, concepts, and information so that each new element builds on the previous element and creates a unified whole?

- How will I "hook" my reader's interest? I might:

  > start with an attention-grabbing statement

  > begin with an intriguing question

  > use descriptive words to set a scene

Below are two strategies to help you introduce your precise claim and topic clearly in an introduction:

- Peer Discussion

  > Talk about your topic with a partner, explaining what you already know and your ideas about your topic.

  > Write notes about the ideas you have discussed and any new questions you may have.

  > Review your notes, and think about what your claim or controlling idea will be.

  > Briefly state your precise and informative claim, establishing why it is important.

  > Write a possible "hook."

- Freewriting

  > Freewrite for 10 minutes about your topic. Don't worry about grammar, punctuation, or having fully formed ideas. The point of freewriting is to discover ideas.

  > Review your notes, and think about what your claim or controlling idea will be.

  > Briefly state your precise and informative claim, establishing why it is important.

  > Write a possible "hook."

Copyright © BookheadEd Learning, LLC

Please note that excerpts and passages in the StudySync® library and this workbook are intended as touchstones to generate interest in an author's work. The excerpts and passages do not substitute for the reading of entire texts, and StudySync® strongly recommends that students seek out and purchase the whole literary or informational work in order to experience it as the author intended. Links to online resellers are available in our digital library. In addition, complete works may be ordered through an authorized reseller by filling out and returning to StudySync® the order form enclosed in this workbook.

YOUR TURN

Choose the best answer to each question about the following introduction from a previous draft of Monica's personal essay.

> Growing up, I was always quiet. I preferred reading books and writing furiously in my notebook over joining neighborhood baseball games and talking loudly at family parties. People would always comment on how quiet I was and I started to think that something was wrong with me. In high school, though, I found an activity that allowed me to use my quieter skills. Soon I learned that there were other people who thought like me.

1. Which sentence could Monica add to the beginning of the paragraph to help her engage her audience's attention?
   - ○ A. My weakness has always been my quiet personality.
   - ○ B. My personality is way different from the rest of my family's.
   - ○ C. Do you think journalists are loud people or quiet people like me?
   - ○ D. Do you ever feel like you are the only person who thinks the way you do?

2. Identify the best sentence that Monica could add to the beginning of the introduction to make it clear to the audience why the claim is significant to discuss.

   - ○ A. I have always struggled to explain and defend my shy personality.
   - ○ B. I am blessed that I am able to work alone.
   - ○ C. Most teenagers have friends who move away.
   - ○ D. Do you ever wonder why you are so different from your brothers and sisters?

 WRITE

Use the questions in the checklist to revise the introduction of your personal essay.

Copyright © BookheadEd Learning, LLC

Please note that excerpts and passages in the StudySync® library and this workbook are intended as touchstones to generate interest in an author's work. The excerpts and passages do not substitute for the reading of entire texts, and StudySync® strongly recommends that students seek out and purchase the whole literary or informational work in order to experience it as the author intended. Links to online resellers are available in our digital library. In addition, complete works may be ordered through an authorized reseller by filling out and returning to StudySync® the order form enclosed in this workbook.

Reading & Writing Companion   **145**

Skill:
Transitions

••• CHECKLIST FOR TRANSITIONS

Before you revise your current draft to include transitions, think about:

- the key ideas you discuss
- the major sections of your essay
- the organizational structure of your essay
- the relationships between complex ideas and concepts

Next, reread your current draft and note places in your essay where:

- the organizational structure is not yet apparent
  - > For example, if you are comparing and contrasting two ideas or life experiences, your explanations about how they are similar and different should be clearly stated
- the relationship between ideas from one paragraph to the next is unclear
  - > For example, when you describe a process in sequential order, you should clarify the order of steps using transitional words like *first, then, next,* and *finally*
- your ideas are not creating cohesion, or a unified whole
- your transition and/or syntax is inappropriate

Revise your draft to use appropriate and varied transitions and syntax to link the major sections of your essay, create cohesion, and clarify the relationships between complex ideas and concepts, using the following questions as a guide:

- What kind of transitions should I use to make the organizational structure clear to readers?
- Are my transitions linking the major sections of my essay?
- What transitions create cohesion between complex ideas and concepts?
- Are my transitions and syntax varied and appropriate?
- Have my transitions clarified the relationships between complex ideas and concepts?

Please note that excerpts and passages in the StudySync® library and this workbook are intended as touchstones to generate interest in an author's work. The excerpts and passages do not substitute for the reading of entire texts, and StudySync® strongly recommends that students seek out and purchase the whole literary or informational work in order to experience it as the author intended. Links to online resellers are available in our digital library. In addition, complete works may be ordered through an authorized reseller by filling out and returning to StudySync® the order form enclosed in this workbook.

Copyright © BookheadEd Learning, LLC

↻ YOUR TURN

Choose the best answer to each question.

1. Below is a section from a previous draft of Monica's essay. The connection between the ideas is unclear. What transition should Monica add to the beginning of the third sentence to make her writing more coherent and appropriate for the purpose, topic, and context of her essay, as well as her audience?

> (1) I knew I had to attend the newspaper meeting, but was scared and really didn't want to go. (2) It wasn't what I thought it would be. (3) When I met the other students, I realized how silly I had been.

- ○ A. Eventually
- ○ B. As a matter of fact
- ○ C. On balance
- ○ D. Another key point

2. Below is a section from a previous draft of Monica's essay. The connection between the ideas in the second and third sentences is unclear. What transitions should Monica add to the beginning of the second and third sentences to make her writing more coherent?

> (1) It's impossible to predict what will happen in the future. (2) Walking into the newspaper office, I had no idea what I wanted to do after graduation. (3) I want to study journalism and become a correspondent for a newspaper.

- ○ A. Eventually, Prior to
- ○ B. As a matter of fact, Including
- ○ C. Before, Now
- ○ D. Another key point, In the meantime

✏ WRITE

Use the questions in the checklist to revise your use of transitions in a section of your personal essay.

Copyright © BookheadEd Learning, LLC

Please note that excerpts and passages in the StudySync® library and this workbook are intended as touchstones to generate interest in an author's work. The excerpts and passages do not substitute for the reading of entire texts, and StudySync® strongly recommends that students seek out and purchase the whole literary or informational work in order to experience it as the author intended. Links to online resellers are available in our digital library. In addition, complete works may be ordered through an authorized reseller by filling out and returning to StudySync® the order form enclosed in this workbook.

Skill:
Precise Language

••• CHECKLIST FOR PRECISE LANGUAGE

As you consider precise language, domain-specific vocabulary, and techniques related to a complicated subject or topic, use the following questions as a guide:

- What information am I trying to explain to my audience?

- What domain-specific vocabulary is relevant to my topic?

- Have I determined the complexity of the subject matter and whether any words and domain-specific vocabulary need additional explanation?

- How can I use techniques such as metaphors, similes, or analogies to help explain difficult concepts?

- Where can I use more precise vocabulary in my explanation?

Here are some suggestions for using precise language, domain-specific vocabulary, and techniques such as metaphors, similes, and analogies to help make complex topics clear:

- determine your topic or area of study

- determine the complexity of the subject matter and whether any words and domain-specific vocabulary need additional explanation in order to make concepts clear

- replace vague, general, or overused words and phrases with more precise, descriptive, and domain-specific language

- try to use metaphors, similes, or analogies to make information easier to understand

  > an example of an analogy for a scientific concept is *a cell membrane is similar to the bricks that make up the outside of a building*

  > a metaphor such as *there is an endless battle between thermodynamics and gravity* can help readers begin to understand the meaning of *thermodynamics*

Copyright © BookheadEd Learning, LLC

Please note that excerpts and passages in the StudySync® library and this workbook are intended as touchstones to generate interest in an author's work. The excerpts and passages do not substitute for the reading of entire texts, and StudySync® strongly recommends that students seek out and purchase the whole literary or informational work in order to experience it as the author intended. Links to online resellers are available in our digital library. In addition, complete works may be ordered through an authorized reseller by filling out and returning to StudySync® the order form enclosed in this workbook.

⟳ YOUR TURN

Choose the best answer to each question.

1. After reviewing the checklist, a student realizes he needs to revise the statement below by using more precise, domain-specific language. Select the best answer that uses domain-specific language to express the ideas in the underlined portion of the sentence.

> <u>I will be the first person to go to college in my family</u>, so my goal is to become a doctor and give back as much as possible to my parents and my community.

- ○ A. I will attend college before any of my siblings have,
- ○ B. Previously, no one in my family has attended school past high school,
- ○ C. I will be a first-generation college graduate,
- ○ D. A diploma post-high school is a dream no one in my family has realized,

2. After reviewing the checklist, a student decides to use a metaphor or simile to explain his idea in the passage below. Select the best revision of the underlined portion of the passage.

> It is thanks to the efforts of my entire neighborhood that I am the person I am today. <u>For some reason, I feel responsible to my community</u> when I complete my college degree.

- ○ A. Like a bird finally leaving the nest for the first time after being taught how to fly by family and friends, I feel responsible to my community
- ○ B. Like the recipient of a gift who wants to write a thank-you note, I feel responsible to my community
- ○ C. I'm a shooting star in the night sky and a rainbow on a cloudy day, so I feel responsible to my community
- ○ D. I feel responsible to my community, which is like an old book that you keep returning to for more lessons,

Copyright © BookheadEd Learning, LLC

Please note that excerpts and passages in the StudySync® library and this workbook are intended as touchstones to generate interest in an author's work. The excerpts and passages do not substitute for the reading of entire texts, and StudySync® strongly recommends that students seek out and purchase the whole literary or informational work in order to experience it as the author intended. Links to online resellers are available in our digital library. In addition, complete works may be ordered through an authorized reseller by filling out and returning to StudySync® the order form enclosed in this workbook.

YOUR TURN

Complete the chart below by revising a sentence or paragraph from your essay draft.

Instruction	Original Sentence/Paragraph	Revised Sentence/Paragraph
Write a precise description of the topic of your essay.		
Revise a sentence or paragraph to include a metaphor, simile, or analogy to help explain your topic.		
Revise a sentence or paragraph to include more precise vocabulary related to your topic.		

Copyright © BookheadEd Learning, LLC

Please note that excerpts and passages in the StudySync® library and this workbook are intended as touchstones to generate interest in an author's work. The excerpts and passages do not substitute for the reading of entire texts, and StudySync® strongly recommends that students seek out and purchase the whole literary or informational work in order to experience it as the author intended. Links to online resellers are available in our digital library. In addition, complete works may be ordered through an authorized reseller by filling out and returning to StudySync® the order form enclosed in this workbook.

Skill:
Conclusions

••• CHECKLIST FOR CONCLUSIONS

Before you write your conclusion, ask yourself the following questions:

- How can I rephrase the thesis or main idea?
- How can I write my conclusion so that it supports and follows from the information I presented?
- How can I communicate the importance of my topic? What information do I need?

Below are two strategies to help you provide a concluding statement or section that follows from and supports the information or explanation presented:

- Peer Discussion

  > After you have written your introduction and body paragraphs, talk with a partner about what you want readers to remember, writing notes about your discussion.

  > Think about how you can articulate, or express, the significance of your topic in the conclusion.

  > Rephrase your main idea to show the depth of your thinking and support for the information you presented.

  > Write your conclusion.

- Freewriting

  > Freewrite for 10 minutes about what you might include in your conclusion. Don't worry about grammar, punctuation, or having fully formed ideas. The point of freewriting is to discover ideas.

  > Think about how you can articulate, or express, the significance of your topic in the conclusion.

  > Rephrase your main idea to show the depth of your thinking and support for the information you presented.

  > Write your conclusion.

Copyright © BookheadEd Learning, LLC

Please note that excerpts and passages in the StudySync® library and this workbook are intended as touchstones to generate interest in an author's work. The excerpts and passages do not substitute for the reading of entire texts, and StudySync® strongly recommends that students seek out and purchase the whole literary or informational work in order to experience it as the author intended. Links to online resellers are available in our digital library. In addition, complete works may be ordered through an authorized reseller by filling out and returning to StudySync® the order form enclosed in this workbook.

Reading & Writing Companion   151

YOUR TURN

Choose the best answer to each question.

1. The following conclusion is from a previous draft of Monica's essay. Monica would like to add a sentence that addresses how being an introvert is beneficial, not only to her, but to people around her. Which sentence could she add after the last sentence to help achieve this goal?

> Albert Einstein was an introvert and look where that got him—the world's more revered physicist! However, there are obstacles too. People don't often discuss the challenges associated with being an introvert. Perhaps we don't talk about it because we are afraid or we think we won't be taken seriously. I am not sure. The gifts that come from such a personality extend beyond me and can positively impact society as a whole.

- ○ A. All challenges also present opportunities for reflection and growth.
- ○ B. Being an introvert has its constraints and takes immense amounts of determination to overcome.
- ○ C. Like Albert Einstein, I have my talents that could benefit the world if they are given the right space to grow and flourish.
- ○ D. I have learned that my introversion and determination allow me to investigate challenging news stories while being sensitive to the people with whom I speak.

2. The following conclusion is from a previous draft of Monica's essay. Monica would like to add a sentence that addresses the part of the writing prompt about goals for the future. Which sentence could she add after the last sentence to help achieve this aim?

> After my time at the newspaper, I started to trust parts of myself that I used to view as weaknesses. Now my heart, determination, and introverted personality help me tell important, true stories. I can finally see that these qualities are some of my greatest strengths.

- ○ A. I wish I could tell my past self that everything would turn out all right.
- ○ B. Even though we have different interests, I know that Kayla and I will still be friends in the future.
- ○ C. As I leave high school, I know that I have the skills to pursue journalism and tell even more stories, because now I embrace every part of what makes me *me*.
- ○ D. Although my introverted personality can be a weakness, I know that it is my greatest strength as a friend and as a school newspaper reporter.

 WRITE

Use the questions in the checklist to revise the conclusion of your personal essay.

Copyright © BookheadEd Learning, LLC

Please note that excerpts and passages in the StudySync® library and this workbook are intended as touchstones to generate interest in an author's work. The excerpts and passages do not substitute for the reading of entire texts, and StudySync® strongly recommends that students seek out and purchase the whole literary or informational work in order to experience it as the author intended. Links to online resellers are available in our digital library. In addition, complete works may be ordered through an authorized reseller by filling out and returning to StudySync® the order form enclosed in this workbook.

Informative Writing Process: Revise

PLAN	DRAFT	REVISE	EDIT AND PUBLISH

You have written a draft of your personal essay. You have also received input from your peers about how to improve it. Now you are going to revise your draft.

◀◀ REVISION GUIDE

Examine your draft to find areas for revision. Use the guide below to help you review:

Review	Revise	Example
Clarity		
Highlight each example or event. Annotate any places where the connection between the example or event and your main idea is unclear.	Include transition words and explanatory phrases to show how examples and events connect to the main ideas in your essay.	My teachers praised my talent for language but always noted that I am uncomfortable working in groups, especially if my best friend wasn't also involved. Kayla and I have been inseparateable since elementary school.
Development		
Identify ideas or events that might need further explanation for your audience to understand.	Make sure you convey your personal experiences using details that help the reader understand what you were thinking and feeling at the time.	Kayla is friendly and outgoing while I am more reserved. She loves science and working in the community garden on weekends, but I'd much rather curl up with a good book or write a short story.

Please note that excerpts and passages in the StudySync® library and this workbook are intended as touchstones to generate interest in an author's work. The excerpts and passages do not substitute for the reading of entire texts, and StudySync® strongly recommends that students seek out and purchase the whole literary or informational work in order to experience it as the author intended. Links to online resellers are available in our digital library. In addition, complete works may be ordered through an authorized reseller by filling out and returning to StudySync® the order form enclosed in this workbook.

Copyright © BookheadEd Learning, LLC

Review	Revise	Example
Organization		
Review your body paragraphs. Are they coherent? Identify and annotate any sentences within and across paragraphs that don't flow in a clear and logical way.	Rewrite the sentences so they appear in a clear and logical order.	The school's newspaper seemed like a natural fit, so I signed up. ~~After I dragged myself to my first newspaper meeting, though, I quickly realized how silly I had been.~~ Id thought about joining the paper before but was intimidated by the newsrooms Id seen on television and in movies. If I cant handle Sunday night dinner with my extended family, how was I supposed to work amid the hustle and bustle of such a high-stakes environment? After I dragged myself to my first newspaper meeting, though, I quickly realized how silly I had been. ~~The school's newspaper seemed like a natural fit, though, so I signed up.~~
Style: Word Choice		
Identify repetitive words or imprecise words that do not clearly convey your ideas and experiences to the reader.	Replace weak and repetitive words and phrases with more descriptive ones that better convey your ideas.	I ~~would not~~ stubbornly refused to seek other companions. My friend-ship with Kayla ~~always seemed very important to me and I did not feel as comfortable with anyone else~~ always felt like a safety net. With Kayla, I could always be myself. She understood if I needed space and encouraged ~~let~~ me to take care of myself. It ~~didn't feel right~~ felt disloyal to look for other friends when Kayla gave me all the support I needed.

Please note that excerpts and passages in the StudySync® library and this workbook are intended as touchstones to generate interest in an author's work. The excerpts and passages do not substitute for the reading of entire texts, and StudySync® strongly recommends that students seek out and purchase the whole literary or informational work in order to experience it as the author intended. Links to online resellers are available in our digital library. In addition, complete works may be ordered through an authorized reseller by filling out and returning to StudySync® the order form enclosed in this workbook.

Copyright © BookheadEd Learning, LLC

Review	Revise	Example
Style: Sentence Fluency		
Read aloud your writing and listen to the way the text sounds. Does it sound choppy? Or does it flow smoothly? Is the emphasis on important details and events?	Rewrite a key passage, making your sentences longer or shorter to achieve a better flow of writing.	In the following weeks, I began to look forward to newspaper meetings. as much as I ~~also~~ looked forward to my nightly calls with Kayla. My assignments were tough., especially when I had to inter view strangers for a story. Yet my ~~My desire~~ determination to succeed kept me focused., and knowing that I planned to spend ~~I spent~~ time alone to write about each new exspereince kept me motivated.

✏️ WRITE

Use the revision guide, as well as your peer reviews, to help you evaluate your personal essay to determine areas that should be revised.

Copyright © BookheadEd Learning, LLC

Please note that excerpts and passages in the StudySync® library and this workbook are intended as touchstones to generate interest in an author's work. The excerpts and passages do not substitute for the reading of entire texts, and StudySync® strongly recommends that students seek out and purchase the whole literary or informational work in order to experience it as the author intended. Links to online resellers are available in our digital library. In addition, complete works may be ordered through an authorized reseller by filling out and returning to StudySync® the order form enclosed in this workbook.

Skill:
Style

Copyright © BookheadEd Learning, LLC

••• CHECKLIST FOR STYLE

First, reread the draft of your personal essay and identify the following:

- slang, colloquialisms, contractions, abbreviations, or a conversational tone

- places where you could use precise language in order to help inform your readers

- the use of the first-person (*I*) or second person (*you*) or third person (*he, she, they*)

- places where you could vary sentence structure and length, emphasizing compound, complex, and compound-complex sentences

  > for guidance on effective ways of varying syntax, use a reference such as Tufte's *Artful Sentences*

- incorrect uses of the conventions of standard English for grammar, spelling, capitalization, and punctuation

Establish and maintain a formal style in your essay, using the following questions as a guide:

- Have I used academic language when informing my audience and a personal, conversational tone only when appropriate?

- Did I consistently use the same perspective (for example, using third-person pronouns) throughout my essay?

- Have I used varied sentence lengths and different sentence structures? Did I consider using reference sources, such as Tufte's *Artful Sentences,* to learn about effective ways of varying syntax?

  > Where should I make some sentences longer by using conjunctions to connect independent clauses, dependent clauses, and phrases?

  > Where should I make some sentences shorter by separating independent clauses?

- Did I follow the conventions of standard English?

Please note that excerpts and passages in the StudySync® library and this workbook are intended as touchstones to generate interest in an author's work. The excerpts and passages do not substitute for the reading of entire texts, and StudySync® strongly recommends that students seek out and purchase the whole literary or informational work in order to experience it as the author intended. Links to online resellers are available in our digital library. In addition, complete works may be ordered through an authorized reseller by filling out and returning to StudySync® the order form enclosed in this workbook.

⟳ YOUR TURN

Choose the best answer to each question.

1. Below is a sentence from another draft of Monica's essay. How can she rewrite the sentence to eliminate slang and non-academic language?

> School work was a breeze, something that I rocked even when I was young, but high fiving kids in class wasn't my thing.

- ○ A. School work came easy to me, something that I never bombed even when I was young, but celebrating other students or conversing with them wasn't something I felt comfortable doing.
- ○ B. School work was a breeze, something that I excelled at even when I was young, but high fiving kids in class wasn't my thing.
- ○ C. School work came easy to me, something that I excelled at even when I was young, but celebrating other students or conversing with them wasn't something I felt comfortable doing.
- ○ D. School work was easy for me, something that I excelled at even when I was young, but getting to chit-chat with kids in class was more difficult.

2. Below is a section of a paragraph from another draft of Monica's essay. Which of the following sentences uses an inconsistent perspective?

> (1) A female student sat at a computer, silently working on her own individual assignment. (2) She was concentrating. (3) When you walk in, she looks up and offers you a small smile before returning her eyes to her screen. (4) She and I were part of the same team. (5) The newspaper office became a place I love.

- ○ A. Sentence 1
- ○ B. Sentence 2
- ○ C. Sentence 3
- ○ D. Sentence 5

✏ WRITE

Use the checklist to revise a paragraph of your personal essay to establish and maintain a style and tone.

Copyright © BookheadEd Learning, LLC

Please note that excerpts and passages in the StudySync® library and this workbook are intended as touchstones to generate interest in an author's work. The excerpts and passages do not substitute for the reading of entire texts, and StudySync® strongly recommends that students seek out and purchase the whole literary or informational work in order to experience it as the author intended. Links to online resellers are available in our digital library. In addition, complete works may be ordered through an authorized reseller by filling out and returning to StudySync® the order form enclosed in this workbook.

Grammar:
Sentence Variety

One way to create a more interesting style when writing or editing a draft is to vary the syntax, or structure, of sentences.

English sentences have four basic structures: simple sentences, compound sentences, complex sentences, and compound-complex sentences. When writers use only one type of sentence, readers may disengage from the text. This is especially evident when authors rely heavily on simple sentences. However, with a knowledge of sentence structures, writers can employ a variety of sentences. In the example below, the writer has revised for greater sentence variety and improved the flow of the text.

Edited for Sentence Variety	Not Yet Edited for Sentence Variety
Ronald Reagan was born in Illinois. He graduated from Eureka College in 1932 and worked as an actor for nearly three decades before entering politics in the 1960s. Because he was considered an effective speaker, he was asked to give a speech at the 1964 Republican National Convention. This speech made him more popular and contributed to his being elected Governor of California in 1966.	Ronald Reagan was born in Illinois. He graduated from Eureka College in 1932. He worked as an actor for nearly three decades. He entered politics in the 1960s. He was considered an effective speaker. In 1964, he was asked to give a speech at the Republican National Convention. This speech made him more popular. He was elected Governor of California in 1966.

Notice that the writer applies the strategies of coordination and subordination to combine sentences. The edited second sentence combines information from three sentences but is still easy to read and understand because it includes the word *before* to show that the relationship between the three events in Reagan's life is chronological.

Another particularly helpful strategy for constructing effective sentences is using parallelism.

Strategy	Text
Use parallel construction to emphasize ideas that are related and equal in importance through the use of similarly constructed clauses, phrases, or single words.	**Black** and **ageless**, he sat rocking **day in** and **day out** in a mindless stupor, lulled by the monotonous squeak-squawk of the chair. Marigolds

Please note that excerpts and passages in the StudySync® library and this workbook are intended as touchstones to generate interest in an author's work. The excerpts and passages do not substitute for the reading of entire texts, and StudySync® strongly recommends that students seek out and purchase the whole literary or informational work in order to experience it as the author intended. Links to online resellers are available in our digital library. In addition, complete works may be ordered through an authorized reseller by filling out and returning to StudySync® the order form enclosed in this workbook.

Copyright © BookheadEd Learning, LLC

↻ YOUR TURN

1. How were these sentences edited for structure?

> Sample Sentences: The plane landed. The passengers departed the plane. The passengers entered the terminal.
>
> Edited Text: After the plane landed, the passengers departed the plane, and they entered the terminal.

○ A. The sample sentences were combined to create a compound sentence.
○ B. The sample sentences were combined to create a compound-complex sentence.
○ C. The sample sentences were combined to create a complex sentence.
○ D. The sample sentences were combined to create one longer simple sentence.

2. How were these sentences edited for sentence variety?

> Sample Sentences: The graduating class gave a talent show. Some of the students performed. Other students worked behind the scenes.
>
> Edited Text: The graduating class gave a talent show. Some of the students performed, and others worked behind the scenes.

○ A. Two of the sample sentences were combined to create a complex sentence.
○ B. Two of the sample sentences were combined to create a compound-complex sentence.
○ C. Two of the sample sentences were combined to create a simple sentence.
○ D. Two of the sample sentences were combined to create a compound sentence.

3. How were these sentences edited for sentence variety?

> Sample Sentences: I want to work on the project with Michael. He can work quickly. His work is accurate. He is also effective at making decisions.
>
> Edited Text: I want to work on the project with Michael. He can work quickly, accurately, and decisively.

○ A. Three sentences were combined to create a compound sentence.
○ B. Three sentences were combined into a pair of parallel clauses.
○ C. Three sentences were combined to create a series of parallel phrases.
○ D. Three sentences were combined to create a series of parallel adverbs.

Copyright © BookheadEd Learning, LLC

Please note that excerpts and passages in the StudySync® library and this workbook are intended as touchstones to generate interest in an author's work. The excerpts and passages do not substitute for the reading of entire texts, and StudySync® strongly recommends that students seek out and purchase the whole literary or informational work in order to experience it as the author intended. Links to online resellers are available in our digital library. In addition, complete works may be ordered through an authorized reseller by filling out and returning to StudySync® the order form enclosed in this workbook.

Grammar: Basic Spelling Rules I

Rule	Text	Explanation
When adding a suffix that begins with a vowel to a word that ends with a silent *e*, usually drop the *e*. When adding a suffix that begins with a consonant to a word that ends with a silent *e*, keep the *e*.	Therefore begrudging neither augury Nor other **divination** that is thine, O save thyself, thy country, and thy king, Save all from this **defilement** of blood shed. Oedipus Rex	*Divination* drops the final silent *e* of *divine*, because the suffix starts with a vowel. *Defilement* keeps the silent *e*, because the suffix starts with a consonant.
Always keep the original spelling of the word when you add a prefix, even if the prefix causes a double letter.	It is the Nation's resilience, not its rigidity, that Texas sees reflected in the flag—and it is that resilience that we **reassert** today. Texas v. Johnson	The prefix *re-* does not change the spelling of the base word *assert*.
When adding a suffix that begins with *a* or *o* to a word that ends with *ce* or *ge*, usually keep the *e*.	The different accidents of life are not so **changeable** as the feelings of human nature. Frankenstein	The final silent *e* remains after the suffix is added to *change*.
When a word ends in a consonant + *y*, change the *y* to *i* before adding a suffix. Usually, when *i* and *e* appear together in one syllable, the *i* comes before the *e*. However, there are many exceptions to this rule.	The earliest epics date back to a time when most people were illiterate. Recited by poets, probably with musical **accompaniment**, these epics were the **movies** of their day. The Epic and the Epic Hero	The final *y* in *accompany* is changed to *i* when the suffix is added. In *movies*, the *i* comes before the *e*.

Copyright © BookheadEd Learning, LLC

Please note that excerpts and passages in the StudySync® library and this workbook are intended as touchstones to generate interest in an author's work. The excerpts and passages do not substitute for the reading of entire texts, and StudySync® strongly recommends that students seek out and purchase the whole literary or informational work in order to experience it as the author intended. Links to online resellers are available in our digital library. In addition, complete works may be ordered through an authorized reseller by filling out and returning to StudySync® the order form enclosed in this workbook.

⟳ YOUR TURN

1. How should this sentence be changed?

> The typical superhero is the personifycation of masculinity, noted for strength, prowess, endurance, and every other virtue except humility.

- ○ A. The typical superhero is the personification of masculinity, noted for strength, prowess, endurance, and every other virtue except humility.
- ○ B. The typical superhero is the personifycation of masculenity, noted for strength, prowess, endurance, and every other virtue except humility.
- ○ C. The typical superhero is the personifycation of masculinity, noted for strength, prowess, endurence, and every other virtue except humility.
- ○ D. No change needs to be made to this sentence.

2. How should this sentence be changed?

> Shakespeare and his peers inhabited an unstable world in which humans were prey to unknown microrganisms that could swiftly terminate their lives.

- ○ A. Shakespeare and his peers inabited an unstable world in which humans were prey to unknown microrganisms that could swiftly terminate their lives.
- ○ B. Shakespeare and his peers inhabited an unstable world in which humans were prey to unnown microrganisms that could swiftly terminate their lives.
- ○ C. Shakespeare and his peers inhabited an unstable world in which humans were prey to unknown microorganisms that could swiftly terminate their lives.
- ○ D. No change needs to be made to this sentence.

3. How should this sentence be changed?

> Browning writes of loving to the depth and breadth and height of the soul, quietly, yet with a passion that replaces past greifs.

- ○ A. Browning writes of loving to the depth and breadth and hieght of the soul, quietly, yet with a passion that replaces past greifs.
- ○ B. Browning writes of loving to the depth and breadth and height of the soul, queitly, yet with a passion that replaces past greifs.
- ○ C. Browning writes of loving to the depth and breadth and height of the soul, quietly, yet with a passion that replaces past griefs.
- ○ D. No change needs to be made to this sentence.

Copyright © BookheadEd Learning, LLC

Please note that excerpts and passages in the StudySync® library and this workbook are intended as touchstones to generate interest in an author's work. The excerpts and passages do not substitute for the reading of entire texts, and StudySync® strongly recommends that students seek out and purchase the whole literary or informational work in order to experience it as the author intended. Links to online resellers are available in our digital library. In addition, complete works may be ordered through an authorized reseller by filling out and returning to StudySync® the order form enclosed in this workbook.

Grammar: Apostrophes

Rule	Text
Use an apostrophe and an *s* to form the possessive of a singular noun.	Is this the custom in King Arthur**'s** house? The Canterbury Tales
Use an apostrophe and an *s* to form the possessive of a plural noun that does not end in *s*. Do not use an apostrophe in a possessive pronoun.	She had been long enough in bondage to other people**'s** pleasure to be considerate of those who depended on **hers**, and in her bitter moods it sometimes struck her that she and her maid were in the same position, except that the latter received her wages more regularly. The House of Mirth
Use an apostrophe alone to form the possessive of a plural noun that ends in *s*.	And so his sons would do after him, and his son**s'** sons, to the final generation. Grendel
Use an apostrophe and an *s* to form the possessive of a singular indefinite pronoun.	"Depending upon one another**'s** hearts, he had still hoped that virtue were not all a dream." Young Goodman Brown
If two or more partners possess something jointly, use the possessive form for the last partner named.	Simon and Garfunkel**'s** list of hit songs is extensive.
If two or more partners possess something individually, put each one's name in the possessive form.	When it comes to tennis, Venus**'s** and Serena**'s** records speak for themselves.
Use an apostrophe to replace letters that have been omitted in a contraction.	The Irish had a hero something like Arthur, Finn MacCool, and stories of Finn spread to Scotland, but that**'s** as far as they went. Conversation with Geoffrey Ashe re: King Arthur

Copyright © BookheadEd Learning, LLC

Please note that excerpts and passages in the StudySync® library and this workbook are intended as touchstones to generate interest in an author's work. The excerpts and passages do not substitute for the reading of entire texts, and StudySync® strongly recommends that students seek out and purchase the whole literary or informational work in order to experience it as the author intended. Links to online resellers are available in our digital library. In addition, complete works may be ordered through an authorized reseller by filling out and returning to StudySync® the order form enclosed in this workbook.

↻ YOUR TURN

1. How should this sentence be changed?

> New Mexico is a state whose history, cultural traditions, and natural beauty deserve to be better known.

- ○ A. New Mexico is a state who's history, cultural traditions, and natural beauty deserve to be better known.
- ○ B. New Mexicos' is a state whose history, cultural traditions, and natural beauty deserve to be better known.
- ○ C. New Mexico's is a state whose history, cultural traditions, and natural beauty deserve to be better known.
- ○ D. No change needs to be made to this sentence.

2. How should this sentence be changed?

> The reputation of Taos as an artists mecca and Georgia O'Keeffes home helps attract visitors.

- ○ A. The reputation of Taos as an artists mecca and Georgia O'Keeffe's home helps attract visitors.
- ○ B. The reputation of Taos as an artist's mecca and Georgia O'Keeffes home helps attract visitors.
- ○ C. The reputation of Taos as an artists' mecca and Georgia O'Keeffe's home helps attract visitors.
- ○ D. No change needs to be made to this sentence.

3. How should this sentence be changed?

> De Niza's and Estevan's one journey did not, however, yield any discoveries of gold or silver.

- ○ A. De Niza and Estevan's one journey did not, however, yield any discoveries of gold or silver.
- ○ B. De Niza and Estevan one journey did not, however, yield any discoveries of gold or silver.
- ○ C. De Niza's and Estevan's one journey did not, however, yield any discoverie's of gold or silver.
- ○ D. No change needs to be made to this sentence.

Copyright © BookheadEd Learning, LLC

Please note that excerpts and passages in the StudySync® library and this workbook are intended as touchstones to generate interest in an author's work. The excerpts and passages do not substitute for the reading of entire texts, and StudySync® strongly recommends that students seek out and purchase the whole literary or informational work in order to experience it as the author intended. Links to online resellers are available in our digital library. In addition, complete works may be ordered through an authorized reseller by filling out and returning to StudySync® the order form enclosed in this workbook.

Reading & Writing Companion 163

Informative Writing Process: Edit and Publish

PLAN	DRAFT	REVISE	EDIT AND PUBLISH

You have revised your personal essay based on your peer feedback and your own examination.

Now, it is time to edit your personal essay. When you revised, you focused on the content of your personal essay. You probably examined how to improve your introduction and conclusion as well as how to make your writing cohesive. When you edit, you focus on the mechanics of your essay, paying close attention to things like grammar and punctuation.

Use the checklist below to guide you as you edit:

☐ Have I used a variety of sentences?

☐ Have I followed basic spelling rules?

☐ Have I used apostrophes correctly throughout the essay?

☐ Do I have any sentence fragments or run-on sentences?

Notice some edits Monica has made:

- Used an apostrophe to make a contraction

- Corrected a spelling error

- Used a variety of sentences

Copyright © BookheadEd Learning, LLC

Please note that excerpts and passages in the StudySync® library and this workbook are intended as touchstones to generate interest in an author's work. The excerpts and passages do not substitute for the reading of entire texts, and StudySync® strongly recommends that students seek out and purchase the whole literary or informational work in order to experience it as the author intended. Links to online resellers are available in our digital library. In addition, complete works may be ordered through an authorized reseller by filling out and returning to StudySync® the order form enclosed in this workbook.

With each passing day, it became clearer that I didn't ~~didnt~~ have to change who I am in order to be happy. My loyalty, determination, and introverted personality might not be the best qualities ~~qualitys~~ in every situation~~.~~, but it ~~It~~ turned out that they are the perfect recipe for a reporter. Before I walked into the newspaper office, I had no idea what I wanted to do after graduation~~.~~, but now ~~Now~~ I know. I want to study journalism and become a correspondent for a newspaper.

✏ WRITE

Use the questions on the previous page, as well as your peer reviews, to help you evaluate your personal essay to determine areas that need editing. Then, edit your personal essay to correct those errors.

Once you have made all your corrections, you are ready to publish your work. You can distribute your writing to family and friends, hang it on a bulletin board, or post it on your blog. If you publish online, share the link with your family, friends, and classmates.

Copyright © BookheadEd Learning, LLC

Please note that excerpts and passages in the StudySync® library and this workbook are intended as touchstones to generate interest in an author's work. The excerpts and passages do not substitute for the reading of entire texts, and StudySync® strongly recommends that students seek out and purchase the whole literary or informational work in order to experience it as the author intended. Links to online resellers are available in our digital library. In addition, complete works may be ordered through an authorized reseller by filling out and returning to StudySync® the order form enclosed in this workbook.

Fate or Foolishness

FICTION

Introduction

An accident creates a violent element that threatens the planet. Can a human and a computerized bird restore things to normal?

V VOCABULARY

chasm
a deep crack in the surface of the earth

bizarre
extremely strange or odd

collide
to crash together violently

ominous
threatening; suggesting that something bad will happen

calamity
a disaster; an event that causes great harm

☰ READ

NOTES

Copyright © BookheadEd Learning, LLC

1   In those days, every human unit was warned to stay away from the EDGE, the Eastern Dangerous Galaxy Enclosure. The EDGE had existed since the twenty-first century. At that time, a ghastly event happened. An explosion happened aboveground. A vast **chasm** appeared, and tunnels cracked open. The planet shook, releasing blasts of bright, flaming energy that **collided** violently in the atmosphere. Half the planet was destroyed. Since then, no one has entered the area of the catastrophe that we call the singularity. It has an intense gravitational pull, so nothing can escape from it. The EDGE was the barrier set up to isolate the **calamity**.

2   Once upon a midnight dreary, I foolishly believed that I could repair the planet and destroy the EDGE. In those days, human units had created machines that were advanced for their time. The machines were programmed well. They did many things for human units. No longer did the units have to know mathematics. The machines calculated for them. No longer did they need dictionaries. The machines "knew" the definition and spelling of every word.

Please note that excerpts and passages in the StudySync® library and this workbook are intended as touchstones to generate interest in an author's work. The excerpts and passages do not substitute for the reading of entire texts, and StudySync® strongly recommends that students seek out and purchase the whole literary or informational work in order to experience it as the author intended. Links to online resellers are available in our digital library. In addition, complete works may be ordered through an authorized reseller by filling out and returning to StudySync® the order form enclosed in this workbook.

NOTES

But, according to the designers and manufacturers, the machines could not think for themselves.

3   I took a different approach with my experiments. I focused on true "artificial intelligence." I built Lenore, a birdlike thinking machine. At first visitors to my laboratory laughed in mockery. "A raven is such a **bizarre** pet for a scientist!" They did not recognize that Lenore was not a real raven. They could not guess that she would change their existence. I taught Lenore to make decisions. She became my dear friend.

4   This explains why I was standing on a desolate plain near the EDGE. It was a dark and stormy night. Sizzling bits of energy seemed to float above the singularity. No plant, nor tree, nor blade of grass grew on the bleak plain. The earth was scorched and stripped bare. The singularity sucked the energy from all living creatures. Merciless blasts of wind rocked my body, but Lenore rested safely under my jacket. **Ominous** cracking and creaking sounds filled me with terror. Yet, I had come to fulfill my destiny. Perhaps I was correct in my actions. I will never know.

5   The beating of my fearful heart drowned out the relentless sounds of the singularity. I moved as close as I dared to the flashing, rippling nightmare that had ruined my beloved planet. Slowly, with shaking fingers, I opened my jacket. Lenore looked at me, wide-eyed, unafraid. Tonight I would lose my friend forever. Yet, I knew if she were successful, my planet would be healed.

6   I eased Lenore out and placed her on my shoulder. I whispered one final goodbye. Then I shouted, "Lenore, do what you must!" She rose into the turbulent air, strong against the violent wind. Her instructions were simple. She was to fly into the singularity and do what was needed to destroy it. She could think and reason. She would know what to do once inside. She circled twice and flew straight into the center. Suddenly, flames exploded, feeding on the oxygen in the air. I struggled to breathe. Horrid shrieks roared and howled. Time and space flew apart, breaking into a million pieces before slamming back together with an ear-splitting scream.

7   The singularity disappeared. The desolate plain was gone, too. I was standing next to an apple tree, and somewhere a raven was making a cawing sound. Stunned, I began walking, not knowing or caring where I was. I picked an apple from the tree and took a bite. Taking a deep breath I looked around. I was in a beautiful garden. It seemed like now there would be a new beginning.

Copyright © BookheadEd Learning, LLC

Please note that excerpts and passages in the StudySync® library and this workbook are intended as touchstones to generate interest in an author's work. The excerpts and passages do not substitute for the reading of entire texts, and StudySync® strongly recommends that students seek out and purchase the whole literary or informational work in order to experience it as the author intended. Links to online resellers are available in our digital library. In addition, complete works may be ordered through an authorized reseller by filling out and returning to StudySync® the order form enclosed in this workbook.

First Read

Read "Fate or Foolishness." After you read, complete the Think Questions below.

☁ THINK QUESTIONS

1. What is the EDGE? Why does it exist?

    The EDGE is _____.

    It exists because _____.

2. Who is Lenore?

    Lenore is _____.

3. What happens at the end of the story?

    At the end of the story, _____

    _____.

4. Use context to confirm the meaning of the word *calamity* as it is used in "Fate or Foolishness." Write your definition of *calamity* here.

    Calamity means_____.

    A context clue is _____.

5. What is another way to say that something is *ominous*?

    Something is _____

    _____.

Copyright © BookheadEd Learning, LLC

Please note that excerpts and passages in the StudySync® library and this workbook are intended as touchstones to generate interest in an author's work. The excerpts and passages do not substitute for the reading of entire texts, and StudySync® strongly recommends that students seek out and purchase the whole literary or informational work in order to experience it as the author intended. Links to online resellers are available in our digital library. In addition, complete works may be ordered through an authorized reseller by filling out and returning to StudySync® the order form enclosed in this workbook.

Skill:
Analyzing Expressions

Copyright © BookheadEd Learning, LLC

★ DEFINE

When you read, you may find English expressions that you do not know. An **expression** is a group of words that communicates an idea. Three types of expressions are idioms, sayings, and figurative language. They can be difficult to understand because the meanings of the words are different from their **literal**, or usual, meanings.

An **idiom** is an expression that is commonly known among a group of people. For example, "It's raining cats and dogs" means it is raining heavily. **Sayings** are short expressions that contain advice or wisdom. For instance, "Don't count your chickens before they hatch" means do not plan on something good happening before it happens. **Figurative** language is when you describe something by comparing it with something else, either directly (using the words *like* or *as*) or indirectly. For example, "I'm as hungry as a horse" means I'm very hungry. None of the expressions are about actual animals.

••• CHECKLIST FOR ANALYZING EXPRESSIONS

To determine the meaning of an expression, remember the following:

✓   If you find a confusing group of words, it may be an expression. The meaning of words in expressions may not be their literal meaning.

- Ask yourself: Is this confusing because the words are new? Or because the words do not make sense together?

✓   Determining the overall meaning may require that you use one or more of the following:

- context clues

- a dictionary or other resource

- teacher or peer support

✓   Highlight important information before and after the expression to look for clues.

Please note that excerpts and passages in the StudySync® library and this workbook are intended as touchstones to generate interest in an author's work. The excerpts and passages do not substitute for the reading of entire texts, and StudySync® strongly recommends that students seek out and purchase the whole literary or informational work in order to experience it as the author intended. Links to online resellers are available in our digital library. In addition, complete works may be ordered through an authorized reseller by filling out and returning to StudySync® the order form enclosed in this workbook.

⟳ YOUR TURN

Read the following excerpt from "Fate or Foolishness". Then, complete the multiple-choice questions below.

> **from "Fate or Foolishness"**
>
> The beating of my fearful heart drowned out the relentless sounds of the singularity. I moved as close as I dared to the flashing, rippling nightmare that had ruined my beloved planet. Slowly, with shaking fingers, I opened my jacket. Lenore looked at me, wide-eyed, unafraid. Tonight I would lose my friend forever. Yet, I knew if she were successful, my planet would be healed.

1. An example of personification is—

   ○ A. "fearful heart"

   ○ B. "beloved planet"

   ○ C. "shaking fingers"

   ○ D. "planet would be healed"

2. According to context clues in the passage, the meaning of this personification is—

   ○ A. loud

   ○ B. afraid

   ○ C. dangerous

   ○ D. unexpected

3. The figurative meaning of the word *nightmare* in this passage is—

   ○ A. a bad dream

   ○ B. an evil spirit

   ○ C. a difficult task

   ○ D. something scary

4. A context clue that best supports this meaning is—

   ○ A. "moved as close as I dared"

   ○ B. "I opened my jacket."

   ○ C. "Lenore looked at me, wide-eyed, unafraid."

   ○ D. "lose my friend forever"

Copyright © BookheadEd Learning, LLC

Please note that excerpts and passages in the StudySync® library and this workbook are intended as touchstones to generate interest in an author's work. The excerpts and passages do not substitute for the reading of entire texts, and StudySync® strongly recommends that students seek out and purchase the whole literary or informational work in order to experience it as the author intended. Links to online resellers are available in our digital library. In addition, complete works may be ordered through an authorized reseller by filling out and returning to StudySync® the order form enclosed in this workbook.

Reading & Writing Companion   171

Skill:
Conveying Ideas

★ DEFINE

Conveying ideas means communicating a **message** to another person. When speaking, you might not know what word to use to convey your ideas. When you do not know the exact English word, you can try different strategies. For example, you can ask for help from classmates or your teacher. You may use gestures and physical movements to act out the word. You can also try using **synonyms** or **defining** and describing the meaning you are trying to express.

••• CHECKLIST FOR CONVEYING IDEAS

To convey ideas for words you do not know when speaking, use the following learning strategies:

- ✓ Request help.

- ✓ Use gestures or physical movements.

- ✓ Use a synonym for the word.

- ✓ Describe what the word means using other words.

- ✓ Give an example of the word you want to use.

Copyright © BookheadEd Learning, LLC

Please note that excerpts and passages in the StudySync® library and this workbook are intended as touchstones to generate interest in an author's work. The excerpts and passages do not substitute for the reading of entire texts, and StudySync® strongly recommends that students seek out and purchase the whole literary or informational work in order to experience it as the author intended. Links to online resellers are available in our digital library. In addition, complete works may be ordered through an authorized reseller by filling out and returning to StudySync® the order form enclosed in this workbook.

⟳ YOUR TURN

Match each example with its correct strategy for conveying the meaning of the word *destroy*.

Example Options	
A	The person rips up a piece of paper.
B	The person says it is like when you break the screen on your phone.
C	The person uses the similar word *ruin*.
D	The person explains that the word means causing a lot of damage to something.

Strategy	Example
Use gestures or physical movements.	
Use a synonym for the word.	
Describe what the word means using other words.	
Give examples of the word you want to use.	

Copyright © BookheadEd Learning, LLC

Please note that excerpts and passages in the StudySync® library and this workbook are intended as touchstones to generate interest in an author's work. The excerpts and passages do not substitute for the reading of entire texts, and StudySync® strongly recommends that students seek out and purchase the whole literary or informational work in order to experience it as the author intended. Links to online resellers are available in our digital library. In addition, complete works may be ordered through an authorized reseller by filling out and returning to StudySync® the order form enclosed in this workbook.

Close Read

✏ WRITE

PERSONAL RESPONSE: In "Fate or Foolishness," using Lenore to save the planet seemed like a good idea, but it could have ended in failure. Tell about a time you acted on a good idea that ended well, although it could have just as easily ended in disaster. Recount the events from your experience and connect them to details in the story. Pay attention to and edit for spelling patterns.

Use the checklist below to guide you as you write.

☐ What is a risky decision that you made?

☐ Why was your idea or action risky?

☐ How did you feel when it ended well?

☐ How can you connect this to details in 'Fate or Foolishness'?

Use the sentence frames to organize and write your personal response.

A risky decision that I made was _____.

It was risky because _____.

I felt very _____.

It could have ended badly if _____.

Instead it ended well when _____.

Afterward, I felt _____.

Please note that excerpts and passages in the StudySync® library and this workbook are intended as touchstones to generate interest in an author's work. The excerpts and passages do not substitute for the reading of entire texts, and StudySync® strongly recommends that students seek out and purchase the whole literary or informational work in order to experience it as the author intended. Links to online resellers are available in our digital library. In addition, complete works may be ordered through an authorized reseller by filling out and returning to StudySync® the order form enclosed in this workbook.

Copyright © BookheadEd Learning, LLC

A First in Space

INFORMATIONAL TEXT

Introduction

Children often dream about what they want to be when they grow up. Sally Ride turned her dream into a reality, and in the process helped establish a role for women in the field of science. Learn more about Sally

 VOCABULARY

limitation

disadvantage that limits the effectiveness of something or someone

cope

to deal effectively with problems or responsibilities

potential

possible; capable of becoming real

direct

guide, oversee, or manage something, such as a project

candidate

someone competing for a position or prize

 NOTES

☰ READ

1   The word "trailblazer" once referred to someone who explored an area and created a trail to guide those who followed. Today the word refers to a person who is the first to do something. It also describes someone who has ignored **limitations** and opened a new path. Sally Ride was a trailblazer, an amazing one.

2   When Sally Ride was little, she didn't ask for typical toys. Instead, she wanted a chemistry set. She also wanted a telescope to study the sky. She might have even wondered what it would be like to travel in space and look down on Earth. Sally was fascinated by science, and her parents supported and encouraged her. She enjoyed sports and competed in junior tennis tournaments. All of these things worked together as Sally pursued different careers.

3   In 1977, Sally was working on her Ph.D. in physics at Stanford University when she noticed an advertisement in the paper. NASA was looking for **potential** astronauts. Until then, only men had been accepted into the program, and they all had to have been military pilots. Then the rules changed. Scientists and engineers were encouraged to apply and so were women. Sally sent in

Copyright © BookheadEd Learning, LLC

Please note that excerpts and passages in the StudySync® library and this workbook are intended as touchstones to generate interest in an author's work. The excerpts and passages do not substitute for the reading of entire texts, and StudySync® strongly recommends that students seek out and purchase the whole literary or informational work in order to experience it as the author intended. Links to online resellers are available in our digital library. In addition, complete works may be ordered through an authorized reseller by filling out and returning to StudySync® the order form enclosed in this workbook.

her application, along with 8,000 others. Only thirty-five individuals, including six women, were chosen as **candidates** for the program.

4   Being an astronaut means being physically able to **cope** with unusual situations, so the training is challenging. Sally learned parachute jumping and water survival. She learned how to deal with the weightlessness that occurs in a zero-gravity situation. She trained in navigation and radio communications. She became part of a team that built a robotic arm designed to launch and retrieve satellites. The arm was to be used on the shuttle, a vehicle that circled and then returned to Earth.

5   In 1979, Sally was approved for assignment to a flight crew. She would be a mission specialist on board the orbiter *Challenger*. Her responsibilities would involve performing experiments using the robotic arm she designed. While she waited for her scheduled launch, she worked as a communications officer for two other space flights. She sent messages and instructions from mission control to the flight crews.

6   Finally, in 1983, Sally soared into space. Her job was to control the robotic arm and perform the same experiments she had practiced on Earth. Using the arm, she sent several satellites into space. She also retrieved other units from space. Sally was the first American woman astronaut. At 32, she was also the youngest individual to travel into space. She became a role model in a job previously performed only by men, and she was on a grand adventure that shaped her life.

7   Sally's second flight took place in 1984. She then began training for yet another voyage. Sadly, in 1986, the *Challenger* exploded as it took off. Sally was not on the flight, but all upcoming assignments were canceled, including Sally's.

8   In 1987, Sally began teaching and devoted herself to helping students who wanted to study science. She started writing science books for children. She began and **directed** education projects including the EarthKAM, which allowed middle school students to take pictures of Earth from a camera on the International Space Station. In 2001, she co-founded *Sally Ride Science* to encourage girls in science, technology, engineering, and math. The company organizes science festivals, creates publications, and develops science programs for students.

9   Sally was made a member of the National Women's Hall of Fame. She was given the Jefferson Award for Public Service. She received two medals for her space flights. In 2003, she became a member of the Astronaut Hall of Fame where pioneering space travelers are remembered and honored for what they accomplished.

Please note that excerpts and passages in the StudySync® library and this workbook are intended as touchstones to generate interest in an author's work. The excerpts and passages do not substitute for the reading of entire texts, and StudySync® strongly recommends that students seek out and purchase the whole literary or informational work in order to experience it as the author intended. Links to online resellers are available in our digital library. In addition, complete works may be ordered through an authorized reseller by filling out and returning to StudySync® the order form enclosed in this workbook.

Copyright © BookheadEd Learning, LLC

First Read

Read "A First in Space." After you read, complete the Think Questions below.

☁ THINK QUESTIONS

1. Who was Sally Ride? Why was she a role model?

   Sally Ride was _____.

   She was a role model because _____.

2. Write two or three sentences to describe the training Sally Ride did.

   Sally trained by learning _____

   _____.

3. What did Sally Ride do after her time as an astronaut?

   After her time as an astronaut, Sally Ride _____

   _____.

4. Use context to confirm the meaning of the word *potential* as it is used in "A First in Space." Write your definition of *potential* here.

   Potential means_____
   _____.

   A context clue is _____
   _____.

5. What is another way to say that someone *coped* with a difficult situation?

   Someone _____
   _____.

Copyright © BookheadEd Learning, LLC

Please note that excerpts and passages in the StudySync® library and this workbook are intended as touchstones to generate interest in an author's work. The excerpts and passages do not substitute for the reading of entire texts, and StudySync® strongly recommends that students seek out and purchase the whole literary or informational work in order to experience it as the author intended. Links to online resellers are available in our digital library. In addition, complete works may be ordered through an authorized reseller by filling out and returning to StudySync® the order form enclosed in this workbook.

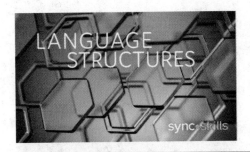

Skill:
Language Structures

★ DEFINE

In every language, there are rules that tell how to **structure** sentences. These rules define the correct order of words. In the English language, for example, a **basic** structure for sentences is subject, verb, and object. Some sentences have more **complicated** structures.

You will encounter both basic and complicated **language structures** in the classroom materials you read. Being familiar with language structures will help you better understand the text.

••• CHECKLIST FOR LANGUAGE STRUCTURES

To improve your comprehension of language structures, do the following:

✓ Monitor your understanding.

- Ask yourself: Why do I not understand this sentence? Is it because I do not understand some of the words? Or is it because I do not understand the way the words are ordered in the sentence?

✓ Break down the sentence into its parts.

- In English, many sentences share this basic pattern: subject + verb + object.

  > The **subject** names who or what is doing the action.

  > The **verb** names the action or state of being.

  > The **object** answers questions such as Who?, What?, Where?, and When?

- Ask yourself: What is the action? Who or what is doing the action? What details do the other words provide?

✓ Confirm your understanding with a peer or teacher.

Copyright © BookheadEd Learning, LLC

Please note that excerpts and passages in the StudySync® library and this workbook are intended as touchstones to generate interest in an author's work. The excerpts and passages do not substitute for the reading of entire texts, and StudySync® strongly recommends that students seek out and purchase the whole literary or informational work in order to experience it as the author intended. Links to online resellers are available in our digital library. In addition, complete works may be ordered through an authorized reseller by filling out and returning to StudySync® the order form enclosed in this workbook.

YOUR TURN

Read each sentence below. Then, complete the chart by identifying the verb and object of each sentence.

Word and Phrase Options					
pursued	wanted	two medals	different careers	received	chemistry set

Sentence	Verb	Object
Instead, **she** wanted a chemistry set.		
All of these things worked together as **Sally** pursued different careers.		
She received two medals for her space flights.		

Please note that excerpts and passages in the StudySync® library and this workbook are intended as touchstones to generate interest in an author's work. The excerpts and passages do not substitute for the reading of entire texts, and StudySync® strongly recommends that students seek out and purchase the whole literary or informational work in order to experience it as the author intended. Links to online resellers are available in our digital library. In addition, complete works may be ordered through an authorized reseller by filling out and returning to StudySync® the order form enclosed in this workbook.

Copyright © BookheadEd Learning, LLC

Skill:
Retelling and Summarizing

★ DEFINE

You can retell and summarize a text after reading to show your understanding. **Retelling** is telling a story again in your own words. **Summarizing** is giving a short explanation of the most important ideas in a text.

Keep your retelling or summary **concise**. Only include important information and key words from the text. By summarizing and retelling a text, you can improve your comprehension of the text's ideas.

••• CHECKLIST FOR RETELLING AND SUMMARIZING

In order to retell or summarize a text, note the following:

✓ Identify the main events of the text.

- Ask yourself: What happens in this text? What are the main events that happen at the beginning, the middle, and the end of the text?

✓ Identify the main ideas in a text.

- Ask yourself: What are the most important ideas in the text?

✓ Determine the answers to the six WH questions.

- Ask yourself: After reading this text, can I answer Who?, What?, Where?, When?, Why?, and How? questions?

Copyright © BookheadEd Learning, LLC

Please note that excerpts and passages in the StudySync® library and this workbook are intended as touchstones to generate interest in an author's work. The excerpts and passages do not substitute for the reading of entire texts, and StudySync® strongly recommends that students seek out and purchase the whole literary or informational work in order to experience it as the author intended. Links to online resellers are available in our digital library. In addition, complete works may be ordered through an authorized reseller by filling out and returning to StudySync® the order form enclosed in this workbook.

Reading & Writing
Companion

181

↻ YOUR TURN

Read the following excerpt from "A First in Space". Then, place the events in the correct order to retell what happened first, next, and last.

---

from "A First in Space"

In 1977, Sally was working on her Ph.D. in physics at Stanford University when she noticed an advertisement in the paper. NASA was looking for potential astronauts. Until then, only men had been accepted into the program, and they all had to have been military pilots. Then the rules changed. Scientists and engineers were encouraged to apply and so were women. Sally sent in her application, along with 8,000 others. Only thirty-five individuals, including six women, were chosen as candidates for the program.

Event Options	
A	NASA encouraged women to apply to become astronauts.
B	Sally Ride was chosen as a candidate for the astronaut program.
C	Sally Ride worked on her Ph.D.

First	Next	Last

Please note that excerpts and passages in the StudySync® library and this workbook are intended as touchstones to generate interest in an author's work. The excerpts and passages do not substitute for the reading of entire texts, and StudySync® strongly recommends that students seek out and purchase the whole literary or informational work in order to experience it as the author intended. Links to online resellers are available in our digital library. In addition, complete works may be ordered through an authorized reseller by filling out and returning to StudySync® the order form enclosed in this workbook.

Copyright © BookheadEd Learning, LLC

Close Read

✏️ WRITE

ARGUMENTATIVE: The author of "A First in Space" calls Sally Ride a trailblazer. Do you agree? Support your opinion with events and evidence from the text. Pay attention to and edit for subject-verb agreement.

Use the checklist below to guide you as you write.

☐ What is a *trailblazer*?

☐ Do you agree that Sally Ride was a trailblazer?

☐ What events and evidence from the text support your opinion?

Use the sentence frames to organize and write your argument.

A *trailblazer* is a person who _____

an area and makes a path for others to follow. I _____

that Sally Ride was a trailblazer. She was the first American _____

astronaut. She was also the _____

person to travel into space for the United States. These facts show that she was a trailblazer because she

was the _____ to do something important.

Please note that excerpts and passages in the StudySync® library and this workbook are intended as touchstones to generate interest in an author's work. The excerpts and passages do not substitute for the reading of entire texts, and StudySync® strongly recommends that students seek out and purchase the whole literary or informational work in order to experience it as the author intended. Links to online resellers are available in our digital library. In addition, complete works may be ordered through an authorized reseller by filling out and returning to StudySync® the order form enclosed in this workbook.

Copyright © BookheadEd Learning, LLC

PHOTO/IMAGE CREDITS:

cover, ©iStock.com/PeopleImages
cover, ©iStock.com/eyewave, ©iStock.com/subjug, ©iStock.com/lvantsov, iStock.com/borchee, ©iStock.com/seb_ra
p. iii, iStock.com/DNY59
p. iv, ©iStock.com/Natalia_80
p. v, ©iStock.com/Natalia_80
p. v, iStock.com/eskaylim
p. vi, ©iStock.com/Natalia_80
p. vi, ©iStock.com/LeeJianbing
p. vi, iStock.com/Tailex
p. vi, iStock.com/NatalieHelbert
p. vi, iStock.com/skynesher
p. vi, iStock.com/imagedepotpro
p. vii, iStock.com/hanibaram, iStock.com/seb_ra, iStock.com/Martin Barraud
p. vii, iStock.com/ThomasVogel
p. ix, iStock/francescoch
p. x, Chimamanda Ngozi Adichie - Taylor Hill/Contributor/FilmMagic/Getty Images
p. x, Mohsin Hamid - Andrew H. Walker/Staff/Getty Images Entertainment
p. x, Franz Kafka - Stringer/Hulton Archive/Getty Archive Photos
p. x, John F. Kennedy - Hank Walker/Contributor/The LIFE Picture Collection/Getty Images
p. x, Anne Lamott - Darryl Bush/Contributor/Hulton Archive/Getty Images
p. xi, Ursula McPike - courtesy of Ursula McPike
p. xi-Dena Simmons - Getty Images North America: Paul Zimmerman/Contributor
p. xi, Elissa Washuta - Photo courtesy of Elissa Washuta
p. xi, Maddie Baden etc - Image credit Emily Smith
p. 0, ©iStock.com/Natalia_80
p. 5, ©iStock.com/Delpixart/
p. 6, ©iStock.com/Delpixart/
p. 7, ©iStock.com/Natalia_80
p. 8, @istock.com/urbancow
p. 10, @istock.com/urbancow
p. 11, ©iStock.com/eskaylim
p. 12, ©iStock.com/eskaylim
p. 13, ©iStock.com/Natalia_80
p. 14, ©iStock.com/bvb1981
p. 19, ©iStock.com/razihusin
p. 26, ©iStock.com/razihusin
p. 27, ©iStock.com/Caval
p. 28, ©iStock.com/Caval
p. 29, ©iStock.com/ThomasVogel
p. 30, ©iStock.com/ThomasVogel
p. 31, ©iStock.com/Martin Barraud
p. 32, ©iStock.com/Martin Barraud
p. 33, ©iStock.com/razihusin
p. 34, ©iStock.com/numbeos
p. 35, Public Domain
p. 39, ©iStock.com/numbeos
p. 40, ©iStock.com/ValentinaPhotos
p. 41, ©iStock.com/ValentinaPhotos
p. 42, @istock.com/urbancow
p. 43, @istock.com/urbancow
p. 45, ©iStock.com/Orla
p. 46, ©iStock.com/Orla
p. 47, ©iStock.com/numbeos
p. 48, ©iStock.com/Milkos
p. 51, ©iStock.com/nortonrsx
p. 54, ©iStock.com/MStudioImages
p. 57, ©iStock.com/Anagramm

p. 61, ©iStock.com/Sjo
p. 64, Getty: NASA/Contributor/Corbis Historical
p. 65, ©iStock.com/Sjo
p. 66, ©iStock.com/Brostock
p. 67, ©iStock.com/Brostock
p. 68, istock.com/pixhook
p. 69, istock.com/pixhook
p. 70, ©iStock.com/DNY59
p. 71, ©iStock.com/DNY59
p. 73, ©iStock.com/Sjo
p. 74, ©iStock.com/SeventyFour
p. 77, ©iStock.com/santypan
p. 80, ©iStock.com/shironosov
p. 83, ©iStock.com/Borut Trdina
p. 87, Education Images/Contributor/Universal Images Group/Getty
p. 96, DNY59/iStock.com
p. 97, Public Domain
p. 102, DNY59/iStock.com
p. 103, ©iStock/Pali Rao
p. 104, ©iStock/Pali Rao
p. 105, ©iStock.com/pixhook
p. 106, ©iStock.com/pixhook
p. 107, ©iStock.com/Orla
p. 108, ©iStock.com/Orla
p. 109, DNY59/iStock.com
p. 110, ©iStock.com/VICHAILAO
p. 115, ©iStock.com/Petar Chernaev
p. 118, ©iStock.com/ollo
p. 121, ©iStock.com/baona
p. 125, iStock.com/hanibaram, iStock.com/seb_ra, iStock.com/Martin Barraud
p. 126, ©iStock.com/Martin Barraud
p. 132, ©iStock.com/ThomasVogel
p. 135, ©iStock.com/gopixa
p. 137, iStock.com/Tevarak
p. 139, ©iStock.com/Martin Barraud
p. 144, ©iStock.com/bo1982
p. 146, ©iStock/Jeff_Hu
p. 148, ©iStock.com/peepo
p. 151, ©iStock.com/stevedangers
p. 153, ©iStock.com/Martin Barraud
p. 156, ©iStock/Fodor90
p. 158, iStock.com/mooltfilm
p. 160, iStock.com/efks
p. 162, iStock.com/BrianAJackson
p. 164, ©iStock.com/Martin Barraud
p. 166, LeeJianbing/iStock.com
p. 167, NatalieHelbert/iStock.com
p. 167, skynesher/iStock.com
p. 167, michaelbwatkins/iStock.com
p. 167, Tailex/iStock.com
p. 167, imagedepotpro/iStock.com
p. 169, LeeJianbing/iStock.com
p. 170, ©iStock.com/Ales_Utovko
p. 172, ©iStock.com/BlackJack3D
p. 174, LeeJianbing/iStock.com
p. 175, ©iStock.com/CelsoDiniz
p. 176, GCShutter/iStock.com
p. 176, Image Source/iStock.com
p. 176, iStock.com
p. 176, Joel Carillet/iStock.com
p. 176, selimaksan/iStock.com
p. 178, ©iStock.com/CelsoDiniz
p. 179, ©iStock.com/BlackJack3D
p. 181, ©iStock.com/eugenesergeev
p. 183, ©iStock.com/CelsoDiniz

Copyright © BookheadEd Learning, LLC

Please note that excerpts and passages in the StudySync® library and this workbook are intended as touchstones to generate interest in an author's work. The excerpts and passages do not substitute for the reading of entire texts, and StudySync® strongly recommends that students seek out and purchase the whole literary or informational work in order to experience it as the author intended. Links to online resellers are available in our digital library. In addition, complete works may be ordered through an authorized reseller by filling out and returning to StudySync® the order form enclosed in this workbook.

studysync®

Text Fulfillment Through StudySync

If you are interested in specific titles, please fill out the form below and we will check availability through our partners.

ORDER DETAILS

Date:

TITLE	AUTHOR	Paperback/ Hardcover	Specific Edition *If Applicable*	Quantity

SHIPPING INFORMATION

Contact:

Title:

School/District:

Address Line 1:

Address Line 2:

Zip or Postal Code:

Phone:

Mobile:

Email:

BILLING INFORMATION   ☐ SAME AS SHIPPING

Contact:

Title:

School/District:

Address Line 1:

Address Line 2:

Zip or Postal Code:

Phone:

Mobile:

Email:

PAYMENT INFORMATION

☐ CREDIT CARD

Name on Card:

Card Number: Expiration Date: Security Code:

☐ PO

Purchase Order Number:

StudySync Text Fulfillment, BookheadEd Learning, LLC
610 Daniel Young Drive | Sonoma, CA 95476